Charlie C. King began to lose herself in the magic of books and the written word from a very young age. Despite being told by her English teacher not to bother going back to sixth form, she did actually gain an education and forged a successful twenty-year career in children's mental health. Having dipped a toe into the world of authoring with this debut, Charlie is now working on her second book and a series of therapeutic children's books.

Born and bred in Wales, Charlie's ambition is to become a mad old woman, dressed in tie-dye and making home-made gin, furiously not giving a shit as she writes new stories and adventures, surrounded by her collection of cockapoos and horses.

WOLFGANG AND THE BABY LUNATIC

CHARLIE C. KING

'Hey. How was school today?' I ask as he jumps into my arms like a cross between a cannon ball and an octopus. I brace to catch him and I breathe in that familiar smell, and all is well with the world again...

'Not good really Mam,' he says.

'Why babe?'.

'Because I'm pretty sure that Martha is a vampire.'

'Really? Why do you think that?' I ask, bemused.

'Because I caught her sucking blood out of her thumb.'

'Oh! Well, I'm sure she just had a papercut babe! I know Martha's mum. I'm quite sure they aren't vampires babe. They seem a really nice family,' I reply, trying to reassure him.

'Yeah Mam. That's what they want you to think.'

Parenting is wonderful, apparently.
I reckon that's also what they want you to think.

'It is easier to ask forgiveness than permission.'
Admiral Grace Hopper

You know how some books have lists and lists of people the author wants to thank for their help in creating their book? This one doesn't. Instead, here are my apologies.

Wolfgang:
I'm sorry that your imbecile of a mother has probably tainted the rest of your life with this ridiculous book. If the worst comes to the worst, we will move away and live our lives under a new identity. I forbid you to read this book until you are at least 38. I love you, incredible amounts. You were the gorgeous heart of solid gold I found in amongst all the shit.

Fernando:
Um, let me know as soon as you are ready to book our Relate sessions. Love you.

Slipalong and **Sunshine**:
Just like all offspring I really wanted to make you proud, so by all means, go round telling all your mates that I'm an author, just might be an idea not tell them what the title of the book is...

Hosenose and **The Criminal Mastermind**:
Sorry, not sorry. Love you.

Tom Hardy:
Thanks for the Bedtime Stories. Love you pal, you are gorgeous, but I wouldn't really leave Fernando for you. Soz.

Author's Note: Pseudonyms

I really like the word pseudonym. Before I even knew that there was actually a word to describe it, I was at it, making up secret and usually insulting nicknames for people in my head. I give pseudonyms to the characters in my story, but you need to know that I've actually done this for years. I used to think everyone did it. Apparently they don't?

The first time I remember doing it, I was a teenager and I was going out with this guy… and, as neurotic and jealous as a fifteen-year-old could be, I took an instant dislike to my boyfriend-at-the-time's ex. I cruelly decided that she reminded me of a grieving dog so I nicknamed her The Bereaved Spaniel. I actually met The Bereaved Spaniel a few years ago through a mutual (unconnected to the boyfriend-we-no-longer-talk-about) friend. She was actually really lovely and so I felt a bit guilty. Full disclosure though, as lovely as she is, to me she still really looks like a spaniel who has lost its master...

Apart from it being a rather nasty hobby of mine, I absolutely have to use pseudonyms in this story, because everything you read in this book is true[1].

I'm hoping pseudonyms will save me from being run over by offended yummy mummies, this strategy might help me to avoid certain death. I haven't even published the book yet and I already get a bit twitchy when I see a yummy mummy in a Range Rover looking in my direction. So I've got to change some details for my own physical protection too.

---

[1] I actually have no evidence that Cruella was married to Harold Shipman, I made that bit up, and actually, I don't know *for a fact* that Tom Hardy will become my second husband, but I'm ready to kick Fernando out, (perhaps permanently, perhaps temporarily, I haven't decided yet) if Tom turned up at my door…

Seriously though, when my work is in the question (I'm slightly less of a dickhead in work), I would never risk the confidentiality of my clients, so I've altered their names and all identifying details. I don't make up nasty names for my clients of course, just my nearest, dearest, and people I don't like very much. I don't mind offending my friends, family and the odd yummy mummy with my nasty nicknames, but I don't much fancy being sued. It would be just my fucking luck to go to the effort of writing and selling this book, just to get sued and end up even more skint...

Quiz. What kind of Mummy Are You?

How many cups of coffee or energy drinks do you drink in a day?

    a)   5 or less
    b)   0
    c)   10 or more

Do you brush your teeth every day?

    a)   Yes of course!
    b)   I have forgotten a few times, but I would never forget to brush my child's teeth.
    c)   Uh I think so? Might have forgotten once or twice?

Would you ever wear clothes with holes in them?

    a)   Definitely not!
    b)   The only holes in my clothes are for my breasts to poke out of for feeding.
    c)   A few. I have been known to permanent marker my leg to try and hide a hole in my leggings.

Do you buy organic food products?

    a)   As much as I can.
    b)   Always. Without fail. And we are vegan.
    c)   Only when it's cheaper than the normal stuff.

How do you feel about breast-feeding?

    a)   Maybe? I like the idea but I'm not sure how I feel about how my boobs will look afterward so I probably wouldn't.
    b)   Is there any other way?[2]

---

[2] I'm pretty fucking sure that breastmilk isn't vegan… grrr.

…ahh I'm joking, I actually have a lot of respect for veganism (when it's not being stuffed down my throat), I just wish I had an iota of the organisation and commitment needed to follow it.

c) I don't care if babies are bottle fed or breastfed, as long as they are fed.

Are you a bit of a twat?

a) Yes
b) Only when it's in the best interests of my child.
c) I try not to be.

What car do you drive?

a) Massive expensive 4x4, that will never drive off-road.
b) People Carrier - a 7 seater is a must!
c) I don't really know. I keep losing it. Just a normal one?

Does your child eat cucumbers?

a) Yes
b) Yes
c) Nope

How is your timekeeping?

a) Pretty perfect. I like to be early.
b) Our routine is scheduled to the minute.
c) Sorry haven't got time answer this question.

How often do you wash your hair?

a) Every day.
b) Only when it's in the best interests of my child.
c) When I remember.

Do you upcycle?

a) Absolutely. My home is a gorgeous vision of shabby chic.
b) Only when it's in the best interests of my child.
c) Upcycling is totally outside of my skill set.

How do you feel about Baby Showers?

- a) Love them! I had 3 baby showers and had a special outfit for each one.
- b) Love them! What could be better than celebrating the miracle of pregnancy and new life?
- c) Urgh. Will there be alcohol?

Have you ever considered giving your child a Toffee Crisp for his tea?

- a) Um, no.
- b) I sincerely hope this a joke.
- c) Absofuckinlutely.

RESULTS

If your answers are mostly As…

It looks as though you are a **Yummy**. I used to wish I was like you. Did you know you scare the shit out other people with your perfect body and messy bun?

If your answers are mostly Bs…

You are possibly a **Scary**. Tone it down a bit sister, FFS, you are terrifyingly good.

If your answers are mostly Cs…

Like me, it appears you are a **Scrummie**. A beautiful idiot who doesn't quite have her shit together but manages all the same.

You probably doubt yourself, every day, like I do.

Don't worry about your upcycling skills. For some of us, it doesn't matter how much love we put into transforming shit old things into beautiful new ones, they still just look like shit old things. The only creative thing about your house is probably the kitchen, which may, like mine, look like a Tracey Emin installation with its precariously piled bits of baby stuff, toys, crayons and colouring books everywhere, my files and books for my studies on every available surface and usually a sink full of last night's pots waiting to be washed… it's your Art.

Like me, you probably don't drive a child-friendly car. I do not and have no intention of ever driving a child friendly car. Because I'm a stubborn twat who doesn't like to conform.

You're far more likely to see me driving an ancient motorbike and sidecar, squinting through a pair of flying goggles, hair blowing in the wind, my son Wolfgang clinging on for dear life, screaming in terror and precariously stuffed in the sidecar.

INTRODUCTION

If my quiz tells you that you are a **Yummy** mummy, I salute you. I wanted to be you for such a tediously long time. I can imagine all those yummy mummies now, glorious, glamorous and breezing through this new motherhood stuff. Thanks for buying my book and sending some much-appreciated pennies my way. But… if you are a yummy mummy, maybe you should get yourself a refund. This is probably not the book for you. You might be best advised to push your luxuriously posh pram back to the posh bookshop, get that refund and look for something more tasteful to read; maybe a book about growing your own organic baby food.

If you are a **Scary**, slam this goddamned book shut now! Go and look for a book of recipes of vegan stuff you can make with an over-production of breastmilk.

Because if you are a **Yummy** or a **Scary**, you just might not get what follows in this book. I'm afraid you will judge me, and believe me, I did enough of that for myself. Actually, I nearly fucking killed myself with judgement, literally.

Ahem. But seriously, thanks for buying this book. Even if you think it is total crap, please, I beg you, help a girl out and tell absolutely all of your friends to buy it anyway. It might mean that I no longer have to feverishly collect a certain supermarket's loyalty points to partake in the finer things in life. Every little helps!

So let me introduce myself… I am **Baby Lunatic**. Well I guess I was. I'm slightly less of a lunatic now. I am an adult who was driven to insanity by having a baby - not, in case you were wondering, a tiny little infant lunatic, which now I've written it down, sounds really weird.

I am an adult who studies and supports people who lose their shit. It's been my job for a long time. A few years ago, I had a baby and, most inconveniently, I lost my own shit. I hid it well because I was under the impression that if you work in mental health you had absolutely no excuse to go potty. I work in the mindboggling world of trauma, mainly working with childhood trauma. I usually work with babies, children, families, teenagers and occasionally adult survivors. I have spent years working with what's termed attachment problems, my clients' difficulties are often a result of a separation, an interruption, or failure in their attachment with their mothers. And while there are often horrifying circumstances involved, like severe neglect and abuse, substance abuse, addiction and children being removed from birth families, I've discovered that occasionally the culprit for interrupting this bonding process can be purely down to the mother suffering from a shithouse of an illness called postnatal depression.

In my time I've worked with a lot of traumatised people. Abuse, neglect, parents being in prison, kids being groomed, exploited, experiencing bereavements or being in care, to name a few examples. This cornucopia of trauma is usually at the root of most of the problems and issues I work with. But, just before I became a parent myself, I began noticing that there was also a group of children and young people for whom were there were no risk factors such as domestic violence, abuse or neglect, and everything for them at home was relatively normal. I began to wonder why this was.

Two themes kept cropping up: traumatic births and postnatal depression (diagnosed or suspected). It began to make me think seriously about the impact of these two factors on the development of a child's ability to form and maintain healthy relationships. And then karma, fate, the laws of the Universe or whichever sadist up there decided they would help me with my research, put me through the same experience.

Ideal… except I didn't realise what was happening to me.

Many of those who know me will be reading my story for the first time. I didn't talk about it. Although thankfully things are changing a bit, we don't talk about mental health nearly enough. Well, I'm talking about it now, because I eventually got most of my shit back together (I didn't have 100% of it to start with to be honest, so I reckon I'm about even).

I'm a survivor of postnatal depression and I want to roar a battle cry for new mothers everywhere. I'm reclaiming words like mental, nuts, lunatic, bat-shit-crazy and I use them with both mirth and the deepest respect. Humour is my sword against the monster that used to live in my head and the ones that I know live inside other people's heads. My choice of career, a miscarriage, suicidal ovaries and an horrific case of imposter syndrome contributed to the growth of that monster.

Eventually, I did get better, thank fuck.

I'd love to tell you that this is an inspirational self-help guide to new motherhood, but it isn't. This is me taking a huge risk, creating a book that describes my emotional shit show of a journey through my own mental health, and I'm risking making a huge fool of myself if it crashes and burns.

These crazy writings and confessions were me getting cheap therapy. Which is probably the greatest irony of my story, because that's how I earn a living. I'm a therapist, and you would have thought I'd know exactly what was going on and what to do to help myself. But I didn't. I'd had a baby, and I found myself swaddled in the grasp of extremely poor mental health… I was terrified, and I couldn't ask for help. A bloody therapist, specialising in child and family mental health at that, but at that time, I didn't realise I was ill. I was about as useful to myself as a one-legged-man in an arse-kicking competition.

I'm really not sure I should be telling you all this. Choosing to write and share all of this this makes me feel quite queasy. I don't know what the future holds. Will admitting to being a part-time basket case destroy my career? Will anyone ever refer clients to me ever again…? More to the point, what will Wolfgang say when he reads it? I dread to think. What the hell…. it's done now. It began from a place of pain, anger and confusion, a strange process which ended up coming from a place of healing. The first draft of this story was literally thousands of words of fury and anger, that this thing had happened to me. But then it became something else. The very act of writing and editing was calming the storm, of going back time and time again, remembering, changing, adding, editing, re-writing. It was a huge journey.

When it became an actual story, I felt like I owed it to the thousands and thousands of women who experience birth trauma and postnatal depression to tell my story, to add my tiny bit of normalisation, if I can claim to do that.

So here it is. This is my story. How I applied the astonishing love I could sometimes feel for my baby within the panic, the understanding I had gained in my work, my natural instincts and my son's biological need to bond with me. I was bat-shit-crazy with a secret postnatal depression I couldn't tell anyone about, yet somehow my baby gave me the strength to put one foot in front of the other. I stuffed him up my t-shirt, threw the nappy bag over my shoulder, and ran the dangerous and painful gauntlet through new motherhood and postnatal depression.

Come and join me (the Lunatic), Wolfgang (the Baby) and Fernando (the Husband). You might also meet my friends, the Scrummies, Sleepless Beauty, The Enforcer, Manykids, Hosenose, Chickenkicker, and Chainsawpixie as they helped me to feel normal. My company of heroes who witnessed the mad shit that happened to me on my journey to post-partum hell and back. Each one joined me for an occasional visit to Newbaby Nuttiville, but I don't think any of them were resident there for as long as I was.

4

Let me show you how I cringed and hid from the other types; the Yummies and the Scarys, feeling disgusting, terrified… and utterly alone. I never believed that this could happen to me, I couldn't bring myself to believe I had postnatal depression, and I certainly couldn't tell anyone… until I began to recover and I realised this can happen to anyone, even a so-called fucking expert (sorry, I feel like a right self-important twat writing the word *expert*). Don't worry, karma had its revenge on this self-important twat. I fell to Earth with a massive bump, and quickly realised that the sun doesn't actually shine out of my arse.

Don't expect hints and tips about baby-rearing. To be honest I remember fuck all about how to get babies to sleep, or teaching them to eat cucumbers. I know as much about getting babies to eat cucumbers as I do about keeping hold of your marbles as a new mother, and although these days I do know a shitload more about postnatal depression, sadly, not one single cucumber has ever passed the lips of my offspring. Not a single morsel of cucumber in six years… and I'm just going to stop there before I start worrying about the symptoms of bloody cucumber deficiency. Anything I did learn about baby sleep or bloody cucumbers, was forgotten in the foggy panic of my sleep-and-sanity-deprived brain. So we are clear I hope, that this book is based simply on my memoirs. A posh word for a collection of scribbles and diary entries I made while going through all this, my transformation into a mother. *Memoirs*. Such a posh word that I feel like I should be wearing long suede gloves and sporting a cigarette holder whilst writing. How reliable these memoirs are? That is debatable, I guess. This book is made up of ramblings written on scraps of paper, emailed to myself, written on the palms of my hands and completely hidden from the world until Wolfgang was about three years old. That's when I started to write all this mad shit in one Word document. I gathered it all together and could clearly see the words penned on days when I was ill. This book is pulled together from those random notes that I found I had written down, sometimes on scraps of paper, sometimes with no memory of writing them. The notes app on my phone was full of little anecdotes of madness. Sometimes I would look at them and wonder who the hell I was when I was writing them. How on earth could it be me?

Until I found a particular scribble on scrap of paper, which was stuffed in my knicker drawer, I had totally forgotten about a certain day. On the day in question, I skated very close to the edge of the abyss. On that day, I nearly ate dandelions from the side of the road, because for a mad moment, I thought this might help me look like an acceptably competent mother. That's how fucking bad it was. I was completely off my trolley with being a new mum and with postnatal depression. Seeing it written on paper brought it all flooding back. It all seemed so serious when I wrote this stuff, so contorted and shameful, so massive, but now there are some bloody funny bits when I read it back to myself, even if at times it's a bit disturbing. I was really deranged at times.

When I became pregnant, I was a successful professional woman, totally committed to the little ones I worked with. I had a pretty uneventful pregnancy and waddled off into the sunset of maternity leave, looking forwards to meeting my baby and enjoying being a mother. I was prepared. I had a great understanding through my work of the process of bonding, attachment and my baby's mental health. Nothing could possibly go wrong. But it did go wrong. I violently fouled those enormous-post-birth knickers… and because it happened to me, it happened to us, and because I couldn't help myself because I went to that place, denial.

Wolfgang is not my son's real name, but one I dearly wish I'd had the guts to give him. After his birth, I was bruised, broken and disenchanted, and I went on to develop severe postnatal depression. I felt horrible feelings, I thought awful things, and probably the most worrying thing for me was that I felt completely disconnected from my beautiful son. My experience and training in trauma didn't help me at all in the early days... not one tiny little itsy-bitsy bit.

For the first three years after Wolfgang was born, I was often completely off my box on caffeine (how nobody knew this is mysterious, especially because I'm like a Duracell bunny on amphetamine when I'm feeling anxious!). Christ Almighty, I must have been wild.

Mad things happened.

I nearly ate dandelions,

I gave Wolfgang a Toffee Crisp for his tea once,

I hid in the supermarket,

I couldn't upcycle,

I drank too much wine.

In fact, I could probably write this entire book purely listing all the crap, insane things I did as a new mother, tearing out my hair in shame in the process. But that isn't really the point of all this. I could have dealt with all of this; I could even have forgiven myself for the Toffee Crisp. I could have rationalised that not everyone is cut out to create beautiful objects out of junk... most normal people are a bit fat after pregnancy... lots of people can't live without caffeine etc. Fuck it, I could have accepted it all. But I couldn't accept any of it. I rejected everything about myself as a mother. Because I had this deformed and cruel monster living in my head. It was born the same day as my son and its name was *postnatal depression*.

When Wolfgang arrived, I felt nothing apart from the nagging sensation that I was broken and defective. Then a bit later, I just desperately wanted to run away from myself and my new responsibilities, but at the same time I desperately needed to cling on to this baby. I was physically and emotionally torn, pulled in opposite directions, my mind overwhelmed with this intricate and excruciating conflict. The fact that I was supposed to know what I was doing was the worst thing of all.

I knew better than most what the risks were of failing. If we didn't bond properly, our relationship could be tainted, a horrible wedge between us which could last as long as I lived. I was terrified that my son's mental health was at stake and to be perfectly honest, my own mental health was the last thing on my mind. Duh. The mental health professional who lost her shit and didn't realise it. She just thought she was crap at everything and not a natural mother.

This shit had got personal.

I thought my job had prepared me for scary shit. It hadn't. I was a neurotic, ashamed, anxiety-ridden Mam, in a bloody scary place.

Now I'm okay, I want to share this with all the others who feel neurotic, ashamed and anxious, and if that's you, then it's okay, make yourself welcome in my story and remember you aren't alone. If you are pretending to be okay, and you aren't okay, it's okay. Neither was I. Very occasionally I'm still not. If you feel as though you might have or had postnatal depression, come with me, take my hand. It's time.

Actually, even without a mental health issue, parenting can seem its own very special brand of madness these days.

In fact, even without being a parent (I hear you too, my life was crazy before), trying to live life is mad, and hard sometimes. Come with me, cry, laugh, scream and I hope maybe it will feel a little bit better.

Oh yes, I recently received a text message from one of my best friend, Sleepless Beauty. I feel better about the Toffee Crisp thing now.

Don't worry about that Toffee Crisp incident, I gave Beastie half an ice pop for lunch today, I have sunk to a new low. SB

x

PART ONE

1

I'll throw chips at you
if you were born in the 80s

My story begins in the 1980s, a golden age when parental guilt didn't even seem to be a thing. Parenting appears to have been more of a hobby back then. The decade where Bernard Matthews made a fortune selling all sorts of shit coated in golden breadcrumbs (alternative producers of ~~chopped lips and arseholes~~ breaded food products are available).

I was born to my parents Sunshine and Slipalong in 1982. We lived in a little house, we weren't rich, but we weren't poor either. I was conceived in the back of a Ford Anglia (just like the flying car in the Harry Potter film), and I was born with a plastic spoon in my mouth, (much as I wish I had come up with this term, it's a quote borrowed from The Who). Sadly, there are no such things as silver spoons in my family.

Scary and wonderful in equal measure, Sunshine is my long-suffering mother. Well known for being the most gorgeous woman in our town back in the day, she really rocked the most amazing 80s fashions. I remember in particular this vision in thigh high boots, crushed purple velvet and huge shoulder pads. So cool. Looking up at her getting ready for a night out, I thought she was the most beautiful woman in the whole world. You do not mess with Sunshine. She's calm and collected 90% of the time, and completely terrifying the other 10%. When she gets pissed off, you run, especially if you work in any capacity in the customer services industry. God help supermarket workers or council tax employees that she disagrees with about the smallest mistake.

I'm pretty sure that there is a higher rate of PTSD in shop employees and public services employees in the area locally, their symptoms caused by dealing with my mother.

Sunshine is the most amazing grandmother and lives and breathes her grandchildren - I'm almost certain she prefers them to her own kids.

Sunshine is extremely talented at decorating, craft, telling people off, baking, sewing and all sorts of stuff that a mother should be good at. Unfortunately, I appear to have been wearing armbands in that particular gene pool. I can't even sew a button on without it coming off again in a few days. Thankfully, she is teaching my niece all these skills, so at least there will be someone to hem my trousers and bake my birthday cakes when Sunshine kicks the bucket. So all is good there.

My dad, Slipalong is called Slipalong because he currently sports one plastic hip and one rubbish one which desperately needs replacing. This may sound like a cruel nickname but since he developed arthritis in his hips I have literally heard about NOTHING else.

He is a massive hypochondriac, but don't tell him I said that. During the Covid pandemic, he swore blind he had it 37 times. I got so fed up of hearing him complain that I made him go for a test on the thirty-seventh time he started moaning. The test made him gag so much that miraculously he developed an immunity to Covid-19.

Because of his wonky hips, the Slipster has also had some spectacular falls. At 6 foot 2 inches he's built like a brick shithouse and having hips that don't work properly means his centre of gravity is not conducive to staying upright. Thankfully these falls so far have been comical but not serious. The other week he literally fell over a field gate and landed face-first into a massive pile of hay. Sadly, I am not usually around to witness these falls, but I was on the phone to my sister once when it happened. They were walking down a hill, midway through a pub crawl that I was supposed to be joining them on later. I was on the phone to her, making arrangements to meet them later, when she started screaming.

'Dad! Dad! Oh my god Dad!'

All I heard next was the most uncontrollable laughing and snorting. According to my sister – about an hour later when she had stopped laughing that is - Dad's legs had started stepping more quickly than his upper body could handle. He couldn't stop, and by now his body had turned sideways. Disaster was imminent. The story is made even funnier by the fact that he and his new girlfriend (she didn't stick around for long after that actually) had linked arms just before he started side-stepping wildly down the hill, and that she was being dragged along with him. It was a very long hill and they were quite near the top, and thankfully he crashed into a gate halfway down, arthritic legs splayed and clinging on for dear life. Just in case you are worried, he was only seriously injured in the pride and relationship departments, physically he was okay, despite almost doing the splits during the gate crash.

I spent a lot of time with my dad in the 80s and 90s, when his hips still worked and pre the hypochondriac-era. I used to go to work with him in the woods, cutting logs and collecting scrap. So as a child, I too was built like a brick shithouse, but with the luck I typically get, I inherited Sunshine's height (she reckons 5' 3" but I'm pretty sure she's only 5' 2" like me). Whilst I beat most of the boys in school at arm wrestling, my body shape was that of a slightly overgrown dwarf (while you are feeling sorry for my Dad being nicknamed Slipalong, please be aware that he thinks it's funny to whistle the seven dwarves hi-fucking-ho song when I'm walking in front of him). Had I have inherited my mum's perfect body shape and my dad's height, I suspect my life would have been very different, possibly gracing catwalks as a child instead of scrap yards.

There were good times and bad times, I've never lived in a dream world. Mostly forgiven and forgotten, my childhood wasn't fairies and rainbows. I learned the horrors of life pretty early, and maybe that's why later on in my life I decided to pursue the career I did…

As a child I was very close to my grandmother, (or Nain in Welsh), who used to work as a mental health nurse. I had convinced myself that nurses were responsible for washing feet, and I had a real issue with feet (I still do actually). I know, I know. I don't know where the notion came from that cleaning people's feet was an integral part of nursing, but that's what I thought, so for that reason I did not want to be a nurse. Stealing Nain's paper cap (nurses used to wear a cap made out of thin cardboard in the 80s), was the closest I ever came to following in her footsteps; I didn't get into mental health until long after she had died, when I was aged nineteen. I know she wanted me to follow in her footsteps and train to be a nurse, I wonder what she would think if she could see me now, not as a nurse but working in mental health as a therapist?

We lived a few miles from where she worked at an old Insane Asylum which was very famous in the area we lived. It's known locally as The Mental. The Mental was a huge Victorian building with lots and lots of history, and for me the most interesting stories were the stories of the inmates (that's what they were called back then) that Nain would tell me. I used to soak up these stories. Stories of last night's suicides whilst she was on duty, and her memories of lobotomies being performed back in the sixties. She told me about the times she had been an attending nurse whilst surgeons literally drilled with hand drills into the heads of inmates. Gruesome and fascinating as the stories were, they didn't scare me because at the time I don't think I realised they were actually true. Two stories did stick with me and for some reason these did actually feel real. White-haired and in their 80s and 90s at the time, there were these two old ladies who had been in The Mental almost their whole lives. They were patients on my Nain's ward. The first had given birth to a baby out of wedlock. She had been caught in the 1920s having fallen pregnant to a married man, hidden by her family in The Mental and had been there ever since, her baby secretly adopted at birth. Nain told me that she probably wasn't mentally ill when she arrived, but that she had become so institutionalised in the following decades that it was deemed unsafe to let her back into the community; her original diagnosis was *Moral Insanity*.

The memory of the second old lady's story touched me as well. She had been locked away for over 70 years. Her diagnosis was *Insanity caused by Childbirth*. After spending so many decades incarcerated in a mental asylum, she was also deemed at too much risk to be released. I remember Nain telling me that both of these women had been treated repeatedly with Electroconvulsive Therapy. Electroconvulsive fucking therapy for having an affair or for experiencing post-natal depression… When I went on to have my own child, my Nain's stories came back to me, and resonated deeply, their meanings becoming terrifying.

From what I've read since, I've discovered that back then, anyone who could persuade two doctors to sign a form declaring insanity, could get an embarrassing or inconvenient relative locked away in an Insane Asylum. Usually, these unfortunates were women, some of whom went on to spend the entirety of the rest of their lives there. Had my son been born a hundred years before he was, it is possible that I would

14

have been locked away in one of these institutions, my son quietly adopted, whilst I was electrocuted and slowly institutionalised over decades of my life.

2
Sleepless Beauty

At the grand old age of two-and-three-quarters, I was innocently sitting in the local café with Sunshine and her friend, when a disgustingly semi-chewed chip hit me square in the face. I think it was about halfway through 1985 (this was before Nain deemed me old enough to start learning about lobotomies), that I first met my best mate Sleepless Beauty.

Tomato sauce, saliva and potato dripping down my face I turned in my highchair to face my attacker. She was 18 months old with a little squashed face and was clearly a crack shot with a missile.

Our mums became good friends and so Sleepless Beauty and I were forced to spend lots of time together as babies. I'm not sure whether we even liked each other that much, but, whatever the reason, I forgave her for the chip incident, and thirty-five years later we are still best mates. You will be glad to hear that she no longer attacks people with chips. Nowadays she launches her attacks with a very sharp tongue and a terrifying tsunami of righteous anger. Needless to say I rarely challenge her head on…

Forced together by our Mums, we spent a lot of that decade together. Sleepless Beauty was usually naked. Everywhere she went, playing in the garden, round the house and even on the front drive of the house, which overlooked the main thoroughfare through our town, she and her sisters paraded around butt naked. I don't know if it was because I was 18 months older or because my mum was so fussy about my clothes, but I remember being scandalised by it. She usually wears clothes now, just in case you were wondering.

Even though she threw her chips at me and we were forced to spend time together when we were kids, these days I would actually choose her to be my wingwoman (is this some sort of Stockholm Syndrome?). Sleepless Beauty is the bossiest person I know, and my surrogate sister. She is solid gold. She would go on to start popping out children in 2006 and has spent most of the time since telling me how tired she is.

We are total opposites, drive each other mad, and have been close since that day in the cafe. I can even overlook the fact that she drives a massive people carrier, I even get in it sometimes, but only when it's dark and I've had a few drinks.

Family legend says that back in the 1980s, Sleepless Beauty was left outside in her pram next to the entrance to Ethel Austin's (a famous shop for the less well-off back in the day – I still have a couple of tops from there and Ethel's shut down a decade ago!). Her mum only realised she'd forgotten her when she got home, running all the way back to the shop to find her still sleeping peacefully outside the shop. The 80s eh? We understood and forgave so much back then. How much more forgiving we were about crap parenting then, eh? When we chucked kids out of the house with a bike and a jam butty, put whisky in babies' bottles, smoked in the house, left them outside for fresh air, occasionally lost them… and you know what, nobody really gave a shit, as long as your kids were still alive, reasonably clean and had full tummies. As long as we didn't talk to strangers who offered to show us puppies or play knock and run in the old people's bungalows, our parents had done a good job. That's how it seems to me anyway.

In 2012 when I would go on to announce my pregnancy, as luck would have it Sleepless Beauty herself became pregnant with her son Beastie, we were two weeks apart. I say luck. I should say *Lack* rather than *Luck*. Of contraception. The bloody idiot was convinced that the 'rhythm method' worked for her, and yet she kept conceiving... After her third child she started using more reliable methods of contraception.

17

She's going to kill me for telling you that.

When she joined me on the pregnancy journey, she was a massive help. She already had two children so pretty much knew the ropes. She is equally determined, caring, clever, scary and beautiful. She has a bit of an anxiety squint at times too. I recognise it because when she's anxious, she blinks with only one eye. She denies it, but it's true. Another fun fact about Sleepless Beauty is that her elbows bend the wrong way. I shit you not. I'd known the girl for 25 years before I noticed. In the pub, I was trying to teach her to play pool one day. I was wondering why she couldn't hold the cue normally. I nearly fainted when I looked at her properly, her elbows pointed towards me in defiance.

3
Hosenose

Later in 1985, just after I turned three, my mother was diagnosed with my sister, Hosenose. She was born in 1986 and I say diagnosed, because my sister was a right pain in my arse from the moment she was born.

In case it's not obvious, her name isn't really Hosenose, but she was born with a very unfortunate curse - her nose is exactly two millimetres bigger than mine (she insists that we measure them on quite a regular basis). She is a bit of a drama queen and one of her favourite moans is about the discrepancies in our nose sizes.

Although now my best friend and permanent member of my crew, at first we didn't get on. Until our twenties, we seriously, seriously didn't get on. She recently told one of my friends that if I had dropped dead when I was fifteen and she was twelve, she would have clapped with joy at the news and then taken a dump on my grave.

… I'll just leave you there for a moment to visualise this. Hosenose squatting at my fifteen-year-old self's funeral, her head tipped precariously forward due to the mammoth weight of her elephantine nose…

I do love Hosenose. I frustrate the hell out of her, I know this. We are complete opposites. She is full of common sense, whilst I am full of rainbows and energy drinks (or wine, depending on what time of the day it is). She is horrendously stubborn, whereas I'm like a loving, energetic, forgetful puppy. We seriously don't understand each other, but we love each other enough to try. We are each other's best mate and nemesis all rolled into one. She's married to Uncle Knobhead and to be fair I couldn't ask for a better brother-in-law. An interesting mixture of Victor Meldrew and an excited puppy like me, Uncle

Knobhead drives her to distraction, in the same way I do. Bloody good uncle to Wolfgang he is too.

As this book gets going, you will learn that an extraordinary amount of mad shit happens to me. And it's not just me; I think it must be genetic because it happens to Hosenose and Uncle Knobhead too. Our family draws melodrama like magnets.

Hosenose in particular is a strong magnet to random chaos; just this week she's managed to detach her bloody kneecap by falling onto the seat of a fairground ride; not off the ride, that I could understand, but into the actual seat, before the ride had even set off! She stepped up onto the seat and crash landed next to her daughter, Loobie, my niece. The fairground attendant was oblivious, belted her in and the ride took off. Tears streaming down her face (tears that thankfully my niece thought were of excitement), the ride was (hilariously in my opinion) called 'The Bounce'. She described to me the ordeal of the ride. The ride bounced up and down in a circle in the air, the double seats on sort of stalks moving up and down quickly to the rhythm of extremely loud dance music. She certainly did bounce around with her injured leg out flapping up and down in front of her. The way she described it was like she was kicking herself in the face with each bounce, totally out of control of her floppy leg. I know I sound mean, but this kind of stuff happens to her all the time. She has been in Accident and Emergency so many times I reckon she could skilfully direct an episode of Holby City.

She got herself stuck in a wardrobe once. I'm not kidding. She was stuck in an overturned wardrobe and she had to be rescued by the <u>actual</u> <u>fucking</u> <u>fire</u> <u>service</u>. They literally had to break into her house and rescue her. Stuck under the wardrobe for over an hour, she had just managed to reach for her mobile phone from her dressing gown pocket, realised there was no credit on her phone to call a family member and so, in her wisdom, she dialled 999. When they answered she asked them to call Sunshine, but policy and procedure dictated that they couldn't do that (is it possible that they already had a policy for people getting stuck under wardrobes with no credit on their phone? Has this happened before?) so they sent a fire engine and a police car to her house. Sunshine, by pure chance, was popping round to my sister's to drop something off. She pulled up in her car to the terrifying sight of the flashing blue lights of two police cars and a fire engine outside my sister's house. She watched from the car in utter shock as four fire officers smashed through Hosenose's front door with one of those ram things. They raced up the stairs and lifted the heavy wardrobe off her. During the fall, and this is probably the funniest fact about this whole debacle, her dressing gown had been pinned wide open by the sides of the wardrobe... the sight they must have been presented with.... This story is probably still being told at fire service Christmas parties as one of the weirdest incidents they've been called out to.

In fact, our predisposition to ridiculousness has actually rendered me and Hosenose a bit famous. One early morning, when I was five months pregnant, my mobile shrilled and woke me up. Disorientated and noticing that it was still pitch-black outside, I answered and it was Hosenose, screeching and totally panic stricken.

'My house. Flooding. Quick, street flooding, come now!'

It had been raining heavily for days. Everyone in the whole world had wrinkly fingers. She ended the call before I could get any sense out of her. Fernando (my husband, oh wait 'til you hear about him!), and I threw on our clothes and raced to her house. The street was a few inches deep in water.

Sleepless Beauty and her gang also live on the same street so we helped them all to move furniture upstairs and put sandbags in strategic places. Unfortunately, despite everyone's best efforts, the street did flood badly. For two hours I ineffectively fought the flood from getting into my sister's place with a mop. When we were thigh-deep in water I finally persuaded Hosenose that we should give up, and that she should come to my house and have a shower. No vehicles were able to get through so we began wading waist deep through the water. Heading for my house, we clung on tight to each other and slowly made our way along the pavement, towards the dry end of the street, where unbeknown to us my auntie was standing there, filming the devastation. She zoomed in on us.

My childhood nickname Chimpy might give you a clue about how I bounce around like a big kid, still unable to resist the draw of an interesting looking tree. On the contrary, Hosenose has a condition called Dyspraxia and, along with some other interesting effects, the condition renders her notoriously clumsy. She falls over anything and everything. Sometimes she finds navigating her way through fresh air a challenge. So you see the clinging on to one another was as much about her ridiculous sense of balance as it was about protecting my five months' pregnant belly.

What happened next has been immortalised on a certain television show – you know the one where you get paid £250 for funny videos? We made it to the top 100 funniest videos of that particular year and so we are featured in the repeats regularly. Without fail, we get phone calls and messages once or twice a year, captioned with the inevitable question.

'Is this you and Hosenose?'

Like one extremely clumsy drowned rat and one fairly pregnant drowned rat, we waded through the water, and I froze. Having been Hosenose's sister for three decades, I could sense what was going to happen next… I could tell from our position that we were near the edge of the road. Unable to see our feet through the murky, rushing water, I suddenly panicked.

I screamed: 'Hosenose! Watch out for the cur…!' I never got to the 'b', because Hosenose suddenly fell off it. She tumbled into the filthy water, almost dragging me with her. All I could see was her hand sticking up out of the water, somehow she managed to save her mobile phone from getting wet. Honestly, her head and everything went under. I tried to drag her out of the water… I truly did. But I had lost all my strength… um, because I was laughing so much.

I think that's why the video is so popular. My sister had her house flooded and almost drowned, and there I was filmed for the whole world to see… laughing. I am evil and will probably go to hell. And everyone I know has seen the video so I can't even deny it. My twisted sense of humour is available for the whole world to see. In my defence, I did drag her out in the end. Feeling like a hero, hiding my snorting laughter and blissfully unaware that my disgusting humour was going to be broadcasted for the world to see, I dragged her to safety…

When Hosenose announced that she was pregnant aged 19, my 23-year-old self would hit the roof. I would rant and rave at her about responsibility and about throwing her career prospects away. How I berated her with my arrogant opinion back then really makes me cringe with shame now. I couldn't believe that she had decided to have a baby so young. But she did, and she managed just fine. It was me, almost a decade later, who would totally lose my shit when I became a mother.

As teenagers we had fought like cat and dog, as young adults we had got closer, but still hadn't understood each other. If there was one positive to take from my horrendous journey through post-natal depression, it's that Hosenose and me suddenly understood each other far better and as a result would grow much closer. Not only as sisters, but as mothers, and shoulder to shoulder she would help me face postnatal depression.

Hosenose and I entered the 1990's with a bang. Well, a punch would probably be more accurate. I was aged 9 and Hosenose was 6, it was New Year's Eve. I remember waking up curled up in a ball on the landing outside my bedroom door. I could hear screaming and shouting. They were shouting at me. My bones rattled as Sunshine shook me to the rhythm of her angry question;

'Why did you punch your sister?!? Why did you punch your sister!?!'

I had no recollection at all of punching my sister and hadn't a clue what had happened.

That was the first time anyone became aware that I am prone to sleepwalking. I don't know who was the most shocked, Sunshine, Hosenose or me. I imagine that being woken up by a thump in the face to be pretty shocking, but waking up curled up on the floor to my parents shouting and accusing me of a violent act I had no recollection of committing, whatsoever, was pretty shocking too. Although I'm still sure that Sunshine has her doubts that I was asleep, I really was. I would go on to sleepwalk well into my mid-30s. Although I didn't assault anyone again, it did get me into trouble a few times. I once woke up in bed with the wrong man, but I'm too embarrassed to tell you about that....

Anyway, words can't convey how important my Hosenose and Sleepless Beauty were in my fight with post-natal depression, once we had grown out of throwing chips and sleep-punching that is.

I might have had a less-than-loving relationship with Hosenose once, and Sleepless Beauty definitely has inside out elbows, but despite all that, when I went on to develop serious mental illness, I was so lucky to be bookended by the two of them, hoisting me up by my knicker elastic.

4
The Criminal Mastermind

The Criminal Mastermind is my baby brother. Half-brother by blood and full brother by choice.

Sunshine and Slipalong had a slightly-messy-but-typical-90s divorce in the early 1990s. They both went on to have new relationships. When I was 13 years old, my Dad went on to have a son with another woman, and this is where The Criminal Mastermind enters the story. It was 1995, I was in my third year at high school. When he was born, I became like a weird third parent to him. I nearly failed my GCSEs because of him. I moved gradually from a being a high 90% student to only just managing my schoolwork, and my grades dropped seriously. For most of the two years after he was born, I probably only attended school half of the time. When I did, I was so knackered from doing so much with him, worrying about getting out of school on time to pick him up from nursery and the laisser-faire attitude that his own mother showed towards him. I worried about him incessantly until he was aged about 15.

When I think back, my whole adolescence was peppered with sleepless nights worrying about him, not attending school myself so I could be there for his days off sick from nursery, school plays and parents' evenings, having to act like a very young teenage mum. It was far too much, far too young.

How much I cared for my brother, how emotionally attached I was to him; I couldn't have loved him anymore if he had come out of my own womb. But I was too young for such an attachment; I wasn't mature enough to not let the massive responsibility of looking after him take over my life. I didn't understand that this wasn't normal.

The most difficult part of this strange sibling/parent relationship was that due to his own dysfunctional relationship with his mother, I was always second best, my brother every time would rather his own mother than me, the poor understudy.

I think I suffered massively with anxiety when my brother was young, and ultimately, we both suffered because of the actions of other people. Every weekend and some weekdays I was left dealing with the screaming and sobbing when she wasn't there for him, trying to cuddle and reassure him with my immature 15-year-old arms, whilst all he wanted was to get away from me and go to her. I wonder now if the rejection I felt from him then scarred me deeply and etched into my teenage mind the potential that I may not be good enough for any child when I later went on to have my own. Now that I understand the language that I didn't have then. I understand, and I feel for that little girl who didn't have a clue what she was doing, trying her best to bring up a little boy who was not her own.

Unfortunately, The Criminal Mastermind would go on to be a teenager and despite my best efforts to try and keep him on the straight and narrow, he became a proper, proper, proper little shit. For a few years he valiantly tried and miserably failed at being a career criminal. In 2013, on the - actual fucking day - my son was born, the little shit was arrested and held in police custody. Everyone was too scared to tell me what had happened at the time, because they knew I would have got off that hospital bed in full labour, driven straight to the police station to sort him out. I didn't find out until the day after my son was born. But by then I would have my own problems to solve, so the little shit stayed locked up for a while longer, until someone else (I forget who) went to pick him up.

The Criminal Mastermind continued to create a name for himself in crime as an idiot, rather than a gangster. He got caught several times, until he realised he was crap at being a criminal and he got a proper job. Now, earning money legally (most of the time) he is a father himself, sharing a beautiful little boy with my gorgeous sister-in-law, Showgirl.

When I became pregnant, I naively thought that my experiences of looking after The Criminal Mastermind would only help me when my own son came along. Practically, I knew how to look after a baby after all. But I seemed to have forgotten about the emotional side of it. It's probably due to my experiences when I was a teenager and The Criminal Mastermind was a baby, that I never wanted a large family. Our bond was probably what I should have had with my own son, but sadly when my son was born, Postnatal depression robbed me of that, at first.

Anyway, before you get out the tissues (plenty of time for that later), I want to tell you, there is something really quite wonderful about a little brother growing into a big, strong man. We think the world of each other and now I think he feels as protective over me as I do over him, it's a very nice relationship that we have, I feel almost as if I have a big brother these days instead of a little one.   Strangely enough, Hosenose and The Criminal Mastermind look like twins. Except Hosenose is about 10 years older than TCM, so imagine twins where one is healthy and one has had a crack addiction for a few years and that kind of looks like them.

Crack cocaine aside, I really do look like the odd one out. They are like a foot taller than me and the bastards both call me the 'runt of the family'. The short-arse jokes are just so fucking hilarious. No. No they're not, you pair of shithouses.

I am aware I have painted my sister as a smug, big nosed, crack addict and my brother as a little shit and pathetic criminal… and I'm not sorry. I am probably coming across as very mean to them both but they are horrible to me too. We

27

regress around each other, regularly get pissed up and do stupid things like only siblings can do. We ground each other and always have each other's back. I do really love them both.

5
The World's Most Handsome Man

'Have you told them how handsome I am?' Fernando enquired, when I mentioned to him that I was writing this particular chapter.

I guess I'd better tell you about the love of my life, Fernando; my husband, father of my son and self-declared love god. He is my absolute rock, the biggest pain in my arse, my soulmate and the butt of most of my jokes. We have a very playful and childish relationship, and he is the perfect tonic to the seriousness I have to face in the other half of my life, which is when I'm at work.

When I met him, I thought he was a bit of an arsehole. We didn't go to the same high school, but his best mate was in the year above.

'Really? You are seeing her? She was a right hippy in school,' said his best friend when Fernando told him about me. I guess I was, my hair was a different colour every month and I nearly got expelled for having my nose pierced. I lived in Dr Martens and wore those skirts that had little mirrors all over them that you might remember if you were a teen in the 90s. I don't think Fernando and I would have looked twice at each other in school, so it's probably best that we didn't meet each other back then!

I was slightly less of a hippy by the time I met Fernando. It was 2001, I was nineteen. I was in bed after a boozy night out, when I woke up from my drunken snoozing to Sleepless Beauty (she wasn't actually Sleepless Beauty then because she hadn't had any kids yet and still got a good 8 hours in) banging on my door. It was about 3am and I was still quite pissed. Insisting I got dressed, she told me we were going to party. I put some clothes on and bemusedly followed her from my flat, down the road and into the most random house I've ever seen. The living room didn't have any furniture in it, just carpenter's tools, and instead of carpet, there was just sawdust on the floor. There were about twenty people dotted around drinking beer, and I could hear music from upstairs. Sleepless Beauty dragged me upstairs into a room full of people all sitting on a bed or in car seats (actual seats taken out of a car) that were randomly dotted around the room. Apart from the bed, the car seats were the only furniture in this strange little house. There was no door on the bedroom and when I went to the bathroom there was only half a toilet seat, literally just the left half of a toilet seat.

Wondering who the hell lived here and why the hell they hadn't removed the other half of the toilet seat instead of just leaving it there, I precariously hovered and had a wee.

Returning to the heart of the party, I gingerly dropped into one of the car seats. Someone handed me a drink, and I looked around. I kind of knew everyone in the room, most of them I knew or recognised from school, all apart from this huge dark-haired guy who was sitting in another car seat opposite me.

'Whose fucking house is this?' I loudly asked Sleepless Beauty.

'Mine,' drawled Fernando, scowling at me, 'Why?'

'Oh…. Uh… Hi!' I said, cringing.

I didn't fancy him at this point. In fact, I was a bit scared of him and generally thought he was a knobhead. The half circle of a toilet seat did nothing to disabuse me of this idea either.

A few weeks later I bumped into him in the local night club. It was so shit we just called it The Club. Horrific place. You knew when it was going to be an interesting night, because when it got really busy, the gross condensation caused by hundreds of pissed sweaty bodies would cause droplets of sweat to plop into your drink.

Fernando was on the dancefloor talking to someone I knew from school. I don't know what possessed me, I must've been out of my fucking mind on Reef and Aftershock, because I marched up to him and said, pointing at him.

'You.' I drawled and pointed, unable to believe what was coming out of my mouth, 'you are walking me home tonight.'

And that was it. A four-month-long one-night-stand ensued. We would bump into each other on Friday or Saturday night, spend it together, do the walk of shame home from each other's houses early in the morning and totally ignore each other when we bumped into each other during the week, embarrassingly usually at the local paper shop, where my cheeks would burn crimson as I studiously ignored him. We regularly had conversations about how we didn't want a relationship. I certainly didn't want a relationship with him.

He was a bit of a twat back in those days, but something kept drawing me to him. Built like a brick shithouse (another one) he had a matching ego which irritated the hell out of me, but I just couldn't resist him. Our first proper public date was a post-one-night-stand trip to a local caff run by my cousin (this isn't unusual; I'm related to approximately every third person I pass on the street in this town). I was mortified when my cousin lit a candle at our table and draped a tea towel over his arm as he served up our bacon butties. By then everyone knew about us, but we were still busy protesting that we weren't a couple. Twelve months later we were living together, and I haven't been able to get rid of him since.

Fernando is called Fernando in this book, because he thinks the name is totally ridiculous. That's totally why I chose it. He sings songs like Handsome Man by Robbie Williams about himself, pretending that he doesn't really mean it (we all know he does), so Fernando sounded like the right name for my husband, an exotic creature who thinks he's a sex god. I'll call his bluff when he dies and play that song at his funeral. Can you imagine??

I had a choice list of pseudonyms for him actually. He is a teacher and once he came home pissed off because one of his students had started calling him Dave (his real name isn't Dave either), just to wind him up. By the end of term, the whole class were calling him Dave and he was answering to it as well. I almost called him Patrick in the early days of writing this book too, a name that our son insisted on calling him for a whole weekend recently. He pretends he doesn't care about this stuff but he so does. The fact he pretends he doesn't care makes it even funnier.

As much as I take the piss out of my long-suffering husband, and I do, on an hourly basis, he really is the love of my life. I would like to say I am also the love of Fernando's life. Sadly, I think I only come a close second to his mountain bike. That's his thing, mountain biking. He bought me a mountain bike once, and it really pisses him off that it doesn't get used very much. It pisses him off even more that when I do go out cycling, I prefer to use this old lady's shopping bike that Slipalong found in a skip and pinched for me. He drives along on his posh bike and I follow with my shopping bike, half the paint is peeling off it and the basket on the front is skew-whiff (I broke the basket carrying home a huge crate of beer and a bottle of gin from Gossip and Groceries last summer – it was hilarious, because of the uneven weight of the crate of beer I was wobbling all over the place, and because of what I was carrying I'm guessing people assumed this wasn't my first alcoholic binge of the day).

He wouldn't be seen dead on my bike, and that makes me like it even more; I always was a sucker for the underdog. His bike is worth three times the value of the shitty car that he drives, whilst mine was free. For me it's a no brainer. Every

Wednesday night, Fernando and his little friends go adventuring up the mountains on their bikes, I piss them off by referring to his little gang as The Secret Seven. They even have matching stickers for their bikes which say *W.N.B.C.* which stands for the Wednesday Night Bike Club, which naturally, I have re-christened Wankers Night Bike Club. He sends me to sleep telling me all about these jumps and tracks and the Strava challenges he and his little friends complete. Fernando is so dedicated to their club that he actually got W.N.B.C. embroidered on his new cycling trainers (I don't know what the fuck he's going to do if a Wednesday becomes inconvenient for any of them??!). He bloody loves his special trainers. His name on the left trainer and W.N.B.C. on the right, apparently these trainers have the stickiest soles in the mountain biking footwear world. I recently had to watch a demonstration of how sticky the soles are as he paraded round the living room, his massive feet flapping around, each step when he lifted his foot sounded like he was velcroed to the laminate flooring. Whilst on the outside I smiled and congratulated him on his special new trainers, inside I was a bit worried. Because whilst Fernando has buckets of enthusiasm for the sport, I'm not sure how skilled he is. In the last two months he has fallen off twelve times, has broken a rib and a metatarsal in his foot. I have alarming visions of him crashing again, but this time because he's somehow stuck the soles of his fucking feet together whilst attempting some stupid stunt on his bike. I imagine him and his bike together in a crumpled mess, everything but his trainers broken, his feet still sole to sole through the frame of his bike. Because of the ridiculous things that happen in my family, I wouldn't even be that surprised. Although Hosenose is the star of that particular show, I reckon the local A& E department have got a book of stupid accidents that happen to people who are connected to me. My grandfather superglued his hand to the pedal of an exercise bike once. He and the whole exercise bike had to be taken to A & E in the back of my Dad's Transit van so they could detach it. I wasn't there but I bet he got some funny looks in the waiting room. So the thought of Fernando crashing his mountain bike because his feet are stuck together is not that far a stretch for my imagination.

Like Superman with Kryptonite, Fernando has a secret weakness. He is a big strong man, reliable, tall, calm, cool and collected. But, in some situations, he.. well, he faints... He swoons like an over-corseted 18th century damsel in distress. It usually happens when he has to face some sort of unpleasant grown-up situation. So far he has fainted because of dentists, a detailed description of his father's piles (you know the ones that come out of your arse?) and funnily enough... caesarean sections make him go a bit weak at the knees too... you can guess what's coming can't you...? It is fucking hilarious, and I guess not a secret at all now I've told all of you. I'll tell you a bit more about that later... although he will deny all knowledge if you ever ask him about it.

To be fair to him he is a star really. Since I was in school I'd had trouble with my periods and hormonal issues, so from day one in our relationship he has had to put up with all the crap that has come alongside that (literal crap sometimes because I've had a dodgy belly since before I met him!) but he's educated himself on my condition, and I secretly think he's a bit of a hero when I overhear him educating others about it. But don't tell him I said that, he's enough of a big head.

6
Bastard The Teenager

Around the time I met Fernando, I managed to score a job as a trainee graphic designer based in a school for children with behavioural problems. It was a fairly responsible job - given that I had just turned 19 years old and still a bit of a knobhead myself[3] – and it was the first step to me forging a career working with troubled children and young people.

After school I had been to college and studied Graphic Design. I wasn't amazing at it but the interviewers at that school seemed to like me. The remit of my job was to spend time with the kids creating projects like magazines, websites and that sort of thing. But I ended up gravitating towards the kids rather than wanting to spend my time behind a computer. When an opportunity came up to train as a youth worker I applied and got the job. I spent the next ten years in different roles working with young people, and, apart from the unsociable hours, I loved it.

I spent most of my twenties in youth work. I worked with teenagers with quite complex needs. I loved the job, I was good at it, and I loved the kids I worked with. Each and every one of them were special. But holy hell, I couldn't ever imagine living in the same house as one. Sunshine, my mother, kindly refers to my teenage years as The Knob-Head Years.

---

[3]My first job was ace too actually. It was after I left school and before I started college. One of my relatives very kindly got me the job, it was maternity cover manning the reception at a local solicitor's office. Literally *all* I had to do all day was welcome in clients and show them through to the relevant office. The rest of the time I just read books. On quieter days I would just spin around on my posh chair, sniffing Tippex if I was really bored. They used to pay me £250 a week which was a fortune to me then. I used to eat posh sandwiches from the deli round the corner, just because I could.

Working with teenagers strengthened my reluctance at the thought of having a family at all, let alone a houseful of kids. As I worked stupid hours, gained my degree and partied most weekends, people around me started having babies. That was about the time that Hosenose told me she was pregnant. She had her first baby at twenty, then they all started having babies! So as well as my younger sister, my mates were now queuing up, happy to scramble up onto this mysterious travellator to motherhood. An uphill travellator, the top of which looked completely unreachable. To me they were like suicidal lemmings. I couldn't understand why they were doing it to themselves. It seemed impossible to be a good parent and be happy at the same time; it was too risky a minefield for me. I felt party to a secret that my sister and my friends didn't. Didn't they know that teenagers were a by-product of children?? It was a weird time. These were the messages my brain was getting from both my gang and my work:

1. If you have a baby, it will turn into a child. If you have a child it will irreversibly, inevitably and selfishly, turn into a teenager.
2. In order to have a baby you must be able to stretch your vagina to the circumference of a watermelon.
3. You are highly likely to shit yourself in labour.
4. From the day your child is born, you are not allowed to sleep for the next three years.
5. Babies turn into children.
6. Um… but didn't you know? Children turn into teenagers.
7. Don't fucking do it. Just DON'T.

I thought I knew more than anyone what teenagers were like. I certainly didn't fancy having one of those!

Can you see why I couldn't see any positives having children, for a very long time? There's no way I could unconditionally love a child and not be heartbroken when said child turned into Bastard the Teenager, who would stink, steal my car/ makeup / clothes / sanity / alcohol and regularly needed picking up from the police station. This is how I saw it back then. I'm aware I'm coming across as a bit of a knob.

I remember joking that condom packets, instead of talking about the most natural feeling, sensual, blah blah blah, should have a picture of a spotty teenager on one side and a people carrier on the other side. Maybe there's still some mileage in this? The strapline could be - *Use me if you don't want either of these!*

Obviously now I realise that my career choice was also part of my reluctance to have children. I wanted kids, but I didn't want all the crap that came with them. Before Wolfgang appeared, I had for almost two decades been surrounded by children and teenagers with awful histories, sad and horrendous backgrounds, and the job changes you as a person. It's changed me, a lot.

Running a youth centre was also pretty hard for me. Apart from the kids there was a lot of responsibility on my young shoulders in managing a building, writing policies and procedures and all that glamourous stuff. I wasn't enjoying it as much as I'd hoped, and after three years the final straw that made me change jobs was this event.

I was summoned by the great and the good to attend a first aid course. I am normally cool in a crisis but I've got a bit of a weak stomach when it comes to bodies, broken bones and especially, leaking body fluids. I always have to fast forward operation scenes in films, that kind of thing. So as there were no real bones broken or burns to tend to on the course, I walked it. I knew how to bandage, create a sling, do CPR on a plastic dummy. I walked out of there feeling pretty confident that if any accidents happened in my youth club, I could deal with it.

And then. And fucking then…

A week later, some little shit that I was responsible for put his fist through a glass window. It was an old Victorian building and the glass just shattered. I marched over to see what the fuss was about. I had grabbed the first aid kit on my way after hearing the glass shattered, in anticipation of an accident. I was trained. I was confident. I was prepared. Fuck me. There were about twenty shards of glass sticking out of his hand pointing in all directions and there was blood everywhere. To my utter shame, I fell to pieces. My vision swam as I saw the carnage. Sweat began beading on my forehead. I dropped the first aid kit on the floor and ran to the toilet. I vomited, leaving the young person bleeding and swearing in the corridor (there was a lot of swearing on both parts, his shouted, mine whispered). I looked in the mirror, threw water over my face. I grabbed the toilet roll, took my phone out of my pocket, and rang for an ambulance. I returned to the boy with the bleeding hand and without looking too closely, I wrapped the whole fucking toilet roll loosely around his hand… the whole toilet roll. I sat with him until the ambulance arrived ten minutes later. Dutifully I rang his parents and they arrived just in time to accompany him and his massive toilet-paper-covered hand in the ambulance.

My training had gone straight out of the window, I hadn't a fucking clue what I was doing. To be honest the only benefit I can now see of wrapping the toilet paper round his hand had been that I could no longer see the injury and disgusting pieces of glass sticking out of his hand in all directions.

At that point, even though I thought that youth work was great, I decided I wanted to do something more specialist (preferably a role which did not include responsibility for grumpy caretakers and bits of broken glass protruding out of kids).

I applied for a new role and was offered it. In the meantime, I needed to get a job because the new contract didn't start for another four months and, by now, Fernando and I had bought a little house and I had bills to pay. How the hell we had even got a mortgage I have no idea. Which fool trusted us to regularly pay that much money for 25 years?? Just a year or so before we had gotten the mortgage, I remember we were so skint (we had spent all our money on alcohol) that we once had to share a sweet chilli flavoured Pot Noodle between us. It was the only thing left to eat in the whole flat.

So, to pay my bills and eat something more substantial than half a pot noodle, I got a job through a friend. I was to become a Residential Support Worker for a company who specialised in young boys displaying sexually harmful behaviour. So I had gone from working in the community with kids on the edge of criminality, often from poverty stricken backgrounds, poorly educated and on the verge of being kicked out of everywhere, to working with kids who were actually legally detained. On my first day, after a quick introduction to the boss and the house manager, I was locked in a room (for my own safety apparently) and given four box files of paperwork to read through. They were full of the history of a boy I was going to be placed with.

The boy was coming up to 18 years old, and the horrific stuff I read in those box files still haunts me, fifteen years later. This boy had been ritually sexually abused by some form of religious cult for over a decade, and then had gone on to abuse younger children. There was a list of offences committed both against and by him, and it chilled me to the bone. On his risk assessment, under the heading Outings, I read;

John is not allowed to be within six feet of any child younger than 5 years old. If John starts to show signs of excitement when out in a public place where children are, such as drooling or rubbing himself, staff must remove John from situation immediately and remind John of his coping skills.

I was about 24 years old at this point, still so young, in fact only 6 or 7 years older than this boy was. I was absolutely gobsmacked at the stuff I read in those files. It was like stuff I had read in the horror fiction that I favoured at the time. But this was real, and a few days later I entered the property for my first shift. Just before that shift started, I had had to go to the office at a different location to collect my ID badge. As I turned to leave, clutching my ID badge, the boss grabbed my wrist on my way out the door and said, 'Always remember, you are dealing with the most dangerous paedophile under the age of 18 in the country. When he's left us next year and gone on to adult services, they won't supervise him like we do. Don't be surprised if you see his name in The Sun, because you probably will see it; he will escape. And he will offend again.'

Armed with this terrifying statement, I arrived at the house for my first shift. I was introduced to the boy. Despite everything I had read and heard, this boy was exactly that. Just a boy. He lived in a semi-detached house with a variety of carers who came and went, always two of us on duty, and usually a manager too. Next door was a young family with two infant children. When they played outside in their garden, they were visible from every window of that house. I'm guessing their parents didn't know about the dangerous boy living next door. I often wonder if anything happened after I left. At 24 years old, only a couple of weeks into the job and not intending to stay - although the company didn't know it, I was only intending to stay until my new contract started - I was in no position to

40

challenge the decision made by managers and company directors way above me, in placing John next door to such young children. I thought it was horrifically wrong, but I was helpless to do anything about it.

The shifts were exhausting. Not the time, even though they were long hours, but because of the hypervigilant state I was always in, trying to protect the general public from a risk they were unaware of, whilst try to look after this young man, and not think about my own feelings. It was nerve-wracking, especially when I was responsible for taking him on outings. After a while I relaxed a bit and began to take more notice of John as a young person, and not just as a danger. I began to realise some things. John didn't dribble because he was lusting after children, he was dribbling because his teeth were fucked. He didn't shit himself in some sort of protest like it was assumed in his paperwork, he shit himself because his bowels were fucked. The sexual abuse he had suffered had damaged him physically and permanently, not to mention emotionally and mentally. This boy was utterly broken.

The realities of just how bad childhoods can be had come startlingly into focus for me. I wanted a baby even less at this point. How on earth was anyone supposed to keep a child safe?

It seemed that I was party to a terrible truth that the new parents around me like Hosenose, Sleepless Beauty and Manykids just didn't know about. I decided at this point that I would make it my mission to become a shit hot auntie to the children around me and hopefully, now I was party to this dark secret, I could help keep my nieces, nephews and the kids of my friends safe from harm. Although I wasn't optimistic. The world at that point seemed like a very scary place, especially for innocent children.

After working for a few weeks with John, he invited me to sit in on a therapy session. John was in intense therapy and saw his therapist three times a week. I was shocked, because I had only just started to work with him. I learned that some children who have been chronically harmed by adults can sometimes trust other adults far too quickly (which perhaps is the opposite of what you would expect), and it's often to their detriment.

I worked with John for four months with that company, and in that time I attended what I seem to remember was four or five therapy sessions. I think a shift happened in me during that time, and watching the therapist work with John, I suddenly knew which direction I wanted my career to head, and it certainly didn't involve my ovaries....

7
The Scarys

…which appeared to be malfunctioning. Maybe my ovaries were reacting to all these babies, and parents and teenagers I was surrounded by. My ovaries certainly weren't twitching (Hosenose says this a lot when she is cuddling other people's babies. I am a visual thinker and I find it incredibly disturbing when she says this). No, my ovaries weren't twitching, it felt more like the fuckers were trying to jump out of my body. The Suicidal Ovaries – now there's a title for a feminist rock band!

I would bleed heavily and experience extreme pain when on my period. I remember first having problems in school. Although I was always knackered with having to look after The Criminal Mastermind all the time anyway, during my period, I would literally fall asleep in my lessons. Biology was the worst. Mrs Doom was a little crooked woman who looked like she should have died 30 years ago. Always angry and with a screeching Dorset accent, I must have been bloody tired to sleep through the racket of her teaching. After a while and a fair few bollockings, she seemed resigned to the fact that I would have to put my head on my arm on my desk and sleep through Biology. During my period I would really struggle to sit in the hard plastic chairs and delightfully high wooden stools they have in science labs. They caused me so much pain that stretching out to put most of my weight on the table was the only way I could relieve the pressure. I would be in agony every month. I didn't know that this wasn't normal. I just thought everyone was like that. In fact, Mrs Doom told me on more than one occasion that I was lazy. I thought everyone had pain like this, and I was just weak and lazy.

Talking about ovaries, whilst mine were trying to self-destruct, other ovaries around the same age as mine were getting very busy. More and more people my age were having babies. People I hadn't seen in years, people I worked with. I was nowhere near ready. I would see people acting pretty normally, albeit looking as if they were trying to hide a beach ball in their jumper. Then they would disappear for a bit. Then they would reappear. And they had changed. Some of them were turning into those types of parents. The Scarys.

Nothing, no Bastard the Teenager, no watermelon-sized vagina, nothing put me off having children as much as this group of people did. The Scarys terrify the shit out of non-parents and parents-to-be with the strange passive-aggressive way they tout membership to Parent Club. I believe this strange initiation process was another part of why I put off having children, and why, when I did, I ended up developing postnatal depression.

Here's a short selection of comments I heard from Scarys before I became pregnant.

'Ooh you've been married for two years now, when are we going to hear the sound of tiny footsteps??'

'You next?!'

'This house is so quiet. It's just not the same without the sound of children's laughter.'

And my personal favourites…

'You better get cracking, time is not on your side, is it??'

I was 28 years old when someone said this to me.

'Bloody hell, nearly 30, you barren or what?' said my husband's cousin. I have no words. He is not even a parent either, he's just a twat… and you know who you are pal.

There's this enormous pressure to get pregnant after you get married. So the magic happens, the wine is flowing, Barry White is crooning, the tadpole valiantly finds the egg, and in a natural miracle worthy of a David Attenborough documentary, life begins… or, from the reaction of the Scarys, life ends.

'Ooh get some sleep now, while you still can'.

Why? Am I never going to sleep again? But you told me to do this!

'Make sure you don't eat too much, your body will be ruined.'

'Use bio-oil on your tummy.'

'Don't bother using those expensive oils on your stomach, waste of money. If you are going to get horrific stretch marks, you're gonna get them. It's just genetics.'

'Don't hate them, be proud! They will be your tiger stripes!'

What the actual fuck? Is my body going to fall to bits? You told me to do this!

'Enjoy your time together while you can, you're going to have your hands full soon!'

What? Do Fernando and me have to wait 18 years for an uninterrupted conversation?

'Ooh make sure you breastfeed, helps you lose all that weight.'

'Don't breastfeed, I did that and now my tits are flat like spaniel's ears.'

It's a very strange situation, one I relate to smokers and ex-smokers. Smokers will often persuade ex-smokers into having just one more fag. You know why?!? So the bastards don't have to stand in the pissing rain by themselves while chuffing away. I actually believe that parents do this too. When you don't have kids there is a huge pressure to have them.

When the magic has happened, when the nappy sniffing game at the baby shower is over (why, oh why the fuck do people do that? Even though I know it's piccalilli in that nappy, I am repeatedly traumatised every time the yellow smeared plastic shit sack comes out), when you are well and truly impregnated, then comes the *Yey! You're in the same club as me now!* In a tone that really means, *ho, ho, ho, you're well and truly fucked now, girl!'*

I really, really, really don't like Baby Showers, I'm a bit creeped out by them. It feels a bit like everyone is crying behind their smiles and really it is a funeral for the mother's old life… for her jeans, boobs, booze, sex, for sleep. At every single one (even now, after becoming a parent myself), I look around and wonder if I come from a different planet. Mind you after this confession I probably won't ever get invited to one again.

Every cloud….

I didn't have a baby shower. Sleepless Beauty and Hosenose didn't even suggest it. Probably because they know how I feel about them. However, my friend Carlsberg recently had what they called a 'gender reveal' party. This is the new thing apparently, an upgraded version of a baby shower. I wasn't invited of course, and I wasn't at all bothered that I wasn't invited, as I assumed the pretend dirty nappies and weird games (and alcohol-free cocktails – which I also don't see the point in whatsoever. Who even drinks these?) would be rolled out. My friends know about my aversion to Baby Showers so it's no surprise I didn't get invited, they probably thought they were doing me a favour. However… When I later saw the photos, my nose was a bit put out of joint, because this particular pre-baby party had taken things to a new level. The gender of the baby was revealed by cannon. Yes. I really said cannon. A fucking cannon! A real exploding cannon which blows pink shit or blue shit out depending on the gender of the baby. Now that's more my kind of thing, a fucking cannon! I can deal with cannons. I cannot deal with nappies filled with piccalilli.

And another thing… Scarys frequent baby showers; they bloody love 'em.

The Scarys have a club which is a bit like Fight Club, except everyone talks about it. You get covered in piss, regurgitated milk and shit instead of blood. A shadowy-eyed but perfectly made up group of people, who are doing their best to look like they are having the best days of their life, at yet another soft play birthday party, where one must curb the craving to steal a chipolata because the food is only for the children. Sometimes that's how I see it anyway. Yeah well, I am a stealer of chipolatas and the one who dared have a glass of wine at the monthly post-baby-massage-lunch (to the outward disgust, perhaps secret envy? of some of the others).

While on the outside of the Scarys Club, from what I saw, in order to be a fully-fledged member, one must transport their tribe in an extra-large people carrier. Sleepless Beauty's people carrier is so big that the kids refer to it as The Bus... (Sleepless Beauty is not a Scary though. If she was, she would have lost her membership a long time ago, purely down to her association with me).

Oh, I see the benefits of the extra space in people carriers, I honestly do. But I can't help it, I bloody hate them. I actually drove one once; a bit of my soul died that day. It was bright green and it looked like a frog. I swore that never, ever would I own one. The absolute horror, the terrifying mid-life crisis - give me a penis shaped BMW any day of the year - that people carriers represented to me.

I shamelessly stereotyped everyone I saw with a people carrier into people who seem to think their children are the absolute epicentre of the whole world. Only the best for little Portia[4] and Monty! I mourned for who they used to be, their individualism. I wondered what car they used to drive. Again, I am aware that I am a complete twat on occasion. Of course, not everyone who drives a people carrier is a Scary. I know, I know.

---

[4]*Portia* was a heroine in Shakespeare's 'The Merchant of Venice', which is pretty cool. But I would just like to point out that as posh-sounding as the name *Portia* is, in Latin it means Pig or Hog.

I couldn't be one of those Scarys. I knew I could never bring a child into this world and never care about anything or anyone else ever again. I couldn't sacrifice my individuality for a people carrier. And I felt guilty for it every time I saw a people carrier. Now of course, I know how it's far healthier for a child to be a big part of a parent's world, but for them to understand that the whole world doesn't revolve around one person.

8
The Job

Sorry got a bit distracted there with The Scarys and my hatred for people carriers. Anyway, the four months working with John were up, and I left that job to start my new contract. I was sad to leave John as he had seemed to trust me, but I can't say I was sad to leave the job. I look back now and wonder just how many adults came and went in this young man's life. I feel really quite shit when I think about John now and the direction in which his life might've gone. I have no facts, just the dubious power of my imagination to guess what happened to him. Thankfully I have never seen his name in the press, which I suppose is positive.

After working with John, a seed of an idea grew in my mind. I wanted to help these kids. My new full time job was working as a complaints officer for children who were in care, and I also worked part-time as an advocate for kids in care. When I was made redundant from my job as a complaints officer (a job title that sounds dry as hell but it was actually very interesting and rewarding), I was offered a small training grant from the government. This was my chance; I applied to do my training as a children's therapist.

I spent the next few years learning how to make a living by understanding human minds and understanding the experiences which shape them. I was learning to be a counsellor to children and young people and I was called a Play and Creative Arts Therapist.

Pretty cool job title, eh? I take a lot of shit about my job, as it indicates that all I do is mess about with Lego and crayons all day long. And, to a certain extent the piss takers are right; I do spend a lot of time covered in glitter and paint. In order to get the kids to work with me I pretend to be a mermaid, or a pirate, or a sea horse or a famous wrestler a whole lot more than your average adult does. To understand them and help them, I have to enter their world, and I do that through the natural language of children, which is play. This is different when it comes to working with teenagers, I don't expect them to pretend to be mermaids and pirates (although they can if they want to), we work a lot with music, art and through a sand tray where they use symbols to represent the different things going on for them.

I have always gravitated towards working with the toughest cases. The kids whose minds and brain structures have been affected by factors like being born addicted to drugs, or into homes where abuse and domestic violence is normal. Some of them have been beaten, starved, raped, groomed, and deserted. I've worked with tiny little child criminals, drug runners, children with convictions for knife and gun crime, twelve-year-olds with convictions for assault, thirteen-year-olds with convictions for sex crimes. Adorable two-year-olds with deliberately broken limbs, children born in squats with no birth certificate; their stories unknown, babies who had somehow managed to survive by eating whatever they could find in the bin. I have worked with little girls pimped out by their mothers, kids who have seen their parents die of drug overdoses, kids who have heard their mother being repeatedly raped and beaten in the next room. I have worked with children tied into their cots, or found eating pet food, I have worked with children left with the lifelong impact of having foetal alcohol syndrome, born addicted to heroin. There were even a couple who had been drugged with methadone by their parents, to keep them quiet. I have worked with hundreds of these children, and most of their stories were terribly distressing.

When I'm working, I enter their little worlds through play, they sometimes aren't just playing the magical, innocent games that you would expect a child to play, no, they are showing me how daddy strangled mummy using a teddy and a skipping rope, they use dragons and monsters to show me fighting social workers who are trying to steal their baby siblings, they show me what they want me to hear by drawing; when it goes well, they eventually learn to trust me and begin to talk to me.

My job is difficult to describe, and those who do know a bit about it have no idea how I can do it, how I can sleep at night. I don't know how I can sleep at night sometimes. Sometimes I can't. But I think what keeps me going is for that hour, once a week, I am completely and utterly there for my little clients. I give it my all. I think if I didn't give it my all, that's when I wouldn't be able to sleep at night, because I would be just another of those adults who have let them down. During that hour, when I'm working, that child becomes the most important child in the world because, often they have never felt like the apple of anyone's eye. God they thrive, it's so heart-warming to see. It's like they learn that 'yes, I can be loved, I am loveable', because sometimes, these children haven't been loved properly by anyone at all. The amount of love shown to me by my clients, especially my little ones is heart-breaking and at the same time extremely precious. I become a trusted adult for them, in a world where many of their adults have not been trustworthy at all. I teach these children to trust adults, and for that hour they are the apple of my eye.

Of course, Wolfgang is truly and utterly the apple of my eye, and always will be. I probably love him even more fiercely because of these other children, in some way maybe on their behalf? This doesn't make sense in my head, but it does in my heart. I think the combination of my work and recovering from postnatal depression has given me a unique perspective in both therapy work and being a parent. It's electric.

9
Tom

You know horror films and horror books? I don't think anything compares to the stories I've heard. But when I see it, actually *see* the evidence of the horrors that these children have experienced, that's a different thing, and I'm sorry to have to ask you to imagine them. But you need to, to understand not only the shit that these kids go through, but what was fuelling my fear of having my own baby. By this time, I'd already met children who had gone through hell, I'd read about awful stuff, I'd heard about awful stuff, but the first time I saw something that really hit me was when I met Tom. I can still see him clearly, and this must have happened at least a decade ago.

I was visiting a foster family and was introduced to Tom. Tom was hobbling around, one of his legs in a plaster cast. Now if you have even had a leg or a foot in plaster, you know how it can affect your balance. It didn't affect Tom's balance at all. He was zooming around the place perfectly well on his tiny, mismatched legs.

Tom's leg had been deliberately broken by one of his parents. The first time Tom's leg was broken, Social Services had not been called as the incident had been passed off as accidental. The second time the leg was broken, Tom had been dropped off at A and E and left there alone by the parents and had ended up being placed in an emergency foster placement.

Sadly, children having deliberately broken limbs isn't that unique an occurrence. Tom's story touched and shocked me because he was so small. He was fifteen months old. Apart from the limping gait, here was also something very strange about Tom. Tom would totally ignore people. He didn't respond to noise at all. He wouldn't make eye contact with anyone or mutter a sound, and he never cried.

My job was to observe Tom, to see where he was at developmentally, and then look at working to help Tom form a bond with his foster carers. Because Tom hadn't bonded with anyone. Apart from violence, Tom had experienced very little of any other sort of interaction with a human being.

The first time I met Tom, I stayed in the background, observing this strange, tiny boy as he hobbled around. I watched him move a heavy dining chair over to the kitchen cupboard, get hold of a tin and then use a tin opener to open the tin. Only fifteen months old, he had somehow developed a strong, extremely dexterous little body in order to survive. By being able to move himself around effectively, by being able to move the chair, by his little fingers managing to operate the tin opener, he showed me exactly what neglect he had suffered.

I worked with Tom and his foster carers for a while, it was fairly successful. Tom learned to smile, occasionally laugh and began to learn there was a chance that not all big humans were going to hurt him. I heard a couple of years later that Tom had been returned to his parents and my faith in the child protection system started to die that day, and I'm sad to say it has never been fully restored.

10
Picnics and Wet Pyjamas

My first client after qualifying (by this time I had already worked 200 supervised sessions on placement) had come to me because she was using a lot of class A drugs. India was thirteen and had already had an abortion. She lived with her mother who had extreme mental health problems. India hadn't been able to engage with a few counsellors who used talking therapy methods, and because she showed an interest in art, she was referred to me.

In her sessions, she created a scene. Week after week the scene was repeated. On one side of the page it was a magical evening scene on a beach. A picnic and a child splashing in the water in the darkness. On the other side of the paper, India would paint large areas in red, swirling her paintbrush creating lovely patterns and then cover it with red glitter. She began to confide in me that this was her as a younger child of about five years old. I read back through some brief notes after the session and realised that India was aged five when she had first come to the attention of social services. Since then she had been in and out of care, returned as soon as Mum's symptoms calmed down a bit and whipped back out again as soon as Mum's mental state began to deteriorate. I always say that it's the stuff that professionals don't know about that worries me, the stuff these kids witness that isn't documented. The stuff they don't talk about. India was working through one of the episodes - which wasn't documented - in her series of drawings of the midnight beach and the huge splashes of red. After several weeks of this, she eventually confided in me that it represented a memory that she hadn't told anyone else about. From what she told me I guessed Mum had to be going through a manic phase at the time. India recalled being woken up by her mother in the middle of the night, and told they were going to the beach.

Mum had packed a picnic of India's favourite sweets and crisps and they got into the car in their pyjamas. India told me about the wonderful time they had had, - and in truth, if it had been daylight and not fuelled by her mother's belief that they had to go at night because the government was watching them during the day - it could have been. She described how she had fallen asleep in the car on the way home, her pyjamas soaking wet after swimming in the sea with her mum.

Sometime later, she had woken up in her own bed feeling cold – as would be expected in wet-through pyjamas – and gone to look for her mum. She found her mum in the bathroom. The huge splashes of red she had been showing me in her paintings represented the blood. Her mother had cut her own wrists with a razor. Blood patches bloomed all around her body on the bathroom floor.

The memory kept coming up in therapy sessions because she couldn't understand the memory and the feelings associated with it. For her, there had been magic and love and excitement, even though she told me she felt cold and soggy in her wet pyjamas. The big pools of blood didn't scare her at first, purely because she didn't know what it was and because they had had such a lovely time a few hours before.

This is the kind of stuff I was working with. You could say I was thrown in the deep end. Story of my life.

11

A Fucking Homeless

'Hi! My name is Baby Lunatic and I'm a therapist, I've been asked by your social worker to maybe spend some time with you, what do you reck…?'

'You?! A fucking therapist? Like a real therapist? You need to get yourself down to New Look Miss, you look like a fucking homeless!'

This delightful young woman who took such an interest in my clothes was my third or fourth proper therapy client since qualifying. We shall call her Kelly. Kelly was fifteen, full of sass and was continually being arrested for violent disorder. A family history chock full of trauma and crime, she was what I guess you would call a hard knock. I wouldn't have wanted a slap from her, she towered above me. She would have bounced me all round that room if she had chosen to. I wasn't convinced that she wouldn't. Clever and intelligent, it was heart-breaking to see that she was unlikely to escape the culture she had grown up with. Kelly had a quick wit and underneath the scary exterior was a little girl who cared deeply for her family. During the time Kelly worked with me, six members of her family, across four generations including her father, were imprisoned for a massive international cocaine smuggling operation.

I was working with kids involved with social services and youth offending services at this time and again I was surrounded not by children and young people who had been cared for and looked after properly, but by neglected, streetwise, excluded young people, many of which would go on to offend as an adult and be imprisoned. I worked with drug-using teens, often self-medicating to help them cope with horrific circumstances. I think the saddest case I ever worked on was with a boy of fourteen called Ivan. Ivan had been caught with a large supply of cannabis. He was riding round on his BMX bike when he was stopped and searched by the police when they found it. He was on a court order to work with the Youth Offending Team, which included me. Ivan didn't attend school; he had been kicked out of all the local ones. Ivan didn't have a mum, she had run off and left him with an abusive father. Ivan hadn't seen her in five years, and it was believed that she was working as a prostitute and using Class A drugs prolifically.

Ivan already had a criminal record for drug running (moving drugs on behalf of dealers who don't want to get their hands dirty – these days they call this process County Lines, which you might have heard about), indecent exposure (he had pulled a moonie at a police car, the police car had stopped and he had been verbally aggressive to the police officer so they booked him), and a firearms offence. I later found out that the firearms offence was that he had shot some crows out of a bedroom window with an air rifle – come on, it's hardly threatening someone with a sawn-off shotgun! In the early 90s I shot Hosenose's space hopper with my dad's air rifle. Nobody thought anything of it then (apart from Hosenose who was very upset, and Sunshine, who gave me yet another massive bollocking). On the surface of things, this kid had some very serious charges. Charges that once were down on paper, meant that his life was basically fucked. Who is going to give you a job if you have drugs, firearms and sexual offices on your record??? What on earth are we doing to these kids?

As I got to know Ivan, I learned that despite his record, there was a very innocent infant inside that rough, tracksuit-wearing, smelly kid. He had never been read to, never baked a cake, been pushed on a swing or tucked in at night. He harboured this fantasy that his mum would come back. He told me that everyone told him that his mum was an 'alcoholic druggie whore', but that he didn't believe them. He told me that he knew one day she would come back for him. He described her to me as a wholesome, loving mother, to whom a terrible injustice had been done which prevented her from seeing her sons.

Ivan's social worker told me that a few years previously, Ivan, his older brother and his Auntie had travelled to the city to see his mum for Christmas Day. On their contact order they were allowed to see their mum for one day per year, Christmas Day. They had taken food, pots and pans, cutlery and everything, because there was nothing in his Mum's flat. They had arrived to find the door hanging off the hinges and pissed or drugged people lying everywhere in the flat. Ivan's mother was not there. They had waited for two hours in that stinking place and she still hadn't turned up. To my knowledge Ivan never saw her again.

Sad as this is, nothing could prepare me for how sad I would feel for him when I discovered that this boy - this motherless, criminal fourteen-year-old boy, who could neither read nor write properly - still believed in Father Christmas. The fact that this boy who was being used as a drug runner, who had probably never even had one nice Christmas, and who I felt was being failed left, right and centre, actually still believed in a childhood magic. How could this possibly be?

How on earth?

In one of his sessions, (it must have been coming up to Christmas time for the subject to come up) he told me that when he was ten, he had woken up on Christmas day and raced downstairs to find no Christmas presents waiting for him. His older brother, in a compassionate flash of protective genius, had tried to protect his younger brother by telling him that Santa doesn't come after the age of 10, and that that meant he was a big boy. The story goes that to celebrate Ivan's coming of age,

the boys had stolen two cans of lager from their still-asleep Dad
and cracked them open for breakfast.

12
The name's Tumble... Mrs Tumble

It's such a weird job, what I do. I know all this stuff that other people don't know about. I work in prisons. I've worked with members of the aristocracy. I've worked with child victims of the most horrifically violent crimes that - if the victims were adults - news reports would be plastered all over the media. But you don't hear about child victims very often and, it makes me feel sick to say this, it's because the papers are only allowed to print stories about serious crimes against children if the child actually dies. If the child survives (which they generally do, because they are surprisingly hardy little things), the general public often have no idea about it. I'm privy to all sorts of highly confidential information. But because play and creativity are my tools to connect with my clients, big and small, I'm often covered in glitter, or wearing some sort of ridiculous hat. I feel like I work for the FBI whilst I have the credibility of Mr Tumble.

Thankfully, there are some angels out there working with these children, they are teachers, social workers and teaching assistants. They understand these children, they understand me and how I work and they don't bat an eyelid at the mad shit I get up to, in my crusade to help children heal.

Just the other day I was working with a little girl, aged six, who has never, ever had any semblance of a childhood. I will call her Letty. From the age of two years old, Letty's life had consisted of being a tiny little mum to her three little brothers who arrived only 9 months apart from each other. I had been working with her for a month and in all that time I had never seen her lose her hypervigilant state of mind in even the smallest giggle. This was peculiar, because I rarely fail to make a child laugh. I am a master of jokes about poo and farting and generally making small children laugh. I am not just a clown though, there is science behind this. Playfulness and laughter is very important in healthy emotional development for children. When we share a laugh about something, we are connecting as humans – because you don't laugh on your own very often do you?[5] My experience tells me that positive human connection is the antidote to negative human interactions, it's really bloody important, so in my work, getting children to laugh is a very serious business. I believe that it's also very difficult for a child to be anxious when I've just done an impression of a constipated chicken or some other such nonsense. So the fact that Letty hadn't laughed yet was perplexing and a bit worrying.

I'd been working with children for two decades, I was working with tiny little humans every day, but for some reason something was different with Letty. Apart from the lack of laughter and letting her guard down there was something else.

I couldn't understand how very *small* this child felt to me. She was no smaller than anyone else in her class, but I had this strange feeling that she is absolutely tiny. Then I realised. Letty had spent most of her life trying to avoid conflict. Domestic violence was rife in her birth home, so to try and protect herself and her little brothers, Letty had made herself as small and insignificant as possible. In reality, for many children growing up in these warzones – because homes where violence is prolific really are like warzones[6] for these poor kids – this would have meant hiding, physically rolling herself up into a ball, that sort of thing. What was happening was that I was empathising with her and sensing how small she felt. So,

[5] Unless you, like me, are a tit who chuckles at their own jokes.

[6] Sadly, brain scans of children who live in chronic domestic violence show the same effects as the brains of returning war veterans. It's that fucking serious, and society barely recognises it.

therapeutically speaking I needed to help her feel big, and to help her feel as though she could relax enough to laugh.

Drastic action was needed... My inner idiot heard the call and woke up. I knew what I needed to do with her, we needed to make a mess.

Mess is part of the course of Play Therapy. Some days it gets very messy. But never had I had a day like this before… In my wisdom I thought it would be a good idea to take in some special inks for marbling art, that Letty might feel more relaxed having had permission to make a mess. I don't usually use materials like marbling inks with the little ones because it is so messy, but Letty needed it. So we did it.

It worked, she started to giggle a tiny bit at the little splashes of ink that hit the table as we created our masterpieces. Splashes that I was comically mopping up, pretending that I was going to get into trouble for making such a mess[7]. It worked. Far too well. Because suddenly one of the ink bottles exploded all over me. I looked like a Smurf. I knew it would take days to get this ink off me, and I'd ruined a good work top. But it didn't matter. Because Letty, this tiny little human, was laughing. She was laughing her little head off. She grabbed my hand and smeared ink all over her own arm, more positive connection, definitely less anxiety, I observed. It was working.

At the end of the session I walked her back to class, and low and behold I got the sense that she had grown a bit, terribly excited about having a blue arm.

I said goodbye and laughed to myself as she ran to show her blue arm to one of her friends. Teaching assistants who don't know me yet stared as I walk past them, looking like an extra from the set of *Avatar*.

---

[7] One of my rules in therapy is that it's impossible for children to get into trouble in the session.

Back in the therapy room I looked around at the mess. I grabbed my phone and called the foster carer to offer to pay for any uniform that the ink may have hit. The foster carer wouldn't hear of it and was just pleased that Letty had begun to connect with me.

The therapy room was covered in greasy blue ink splashes. It was up the walls, all over the table, some had even dripped onto the carpet. I was standing there, face all squished up, contemplating the best cleaning product to get the place sorted when the head teacher came bursting through door asking me to come with her quickly. This head teacher has seen it all and works in one of the most deprived areas in the whole of the UK. She is definitely not a drama queen and so I chased after her knowing that for her to be reacting like this, something really serious must be happening.

She needed my help and so I ran after her up the corridor. I could hear a child shouting.

'Get off me you fucking bitch!!!!'

We reached the small sensory room. On the low sofa was a tiny little boy who although had a very big voice, physically he was almost as small as my previous client.

He was barely being restrained by two teachers.

Bang!

He swung his head and clacked the cheekbone of the teacher on his left.

Ouch! She will probably have a black eye tomorrow I thought to myself, breathing in through clenched teeth. I'll call this little guy Kai.

Kai was tame as a wild animal and his eyes didn't look human whilst he was in that state of utter fear/anger/pain. He hissed and growled and scratched and bit. I've seen it before; behaviour like this doesn't freak me out. It isn't pleasant to see a child in this state, and trained as I am to empathise with them, I

63

feel it right there with them. It kind of hurts me too if that makes sense.

I knew by their faces that the situation was very upsetting for the two women trying to keep Kai safe by holding him.

Taking a deep breath, I entered the room and plonked myself right down on the floor, almost laying down to make sure Kai didn't feel threatened by me. At that point he was in utter fight or flight state, and absolutely couldn't access the higher executive function of his brain. Telling the sofa to calm down at this point would be as effective as telling Kai to calm down.

'Fuck offfffff!' he screams, at nobody in particular.

I start my work by talking nonsense to him and show him my blue arms and the splodges on my face. At this point I was avoiding eye contact and making sure to look down most of the time, just glancing every now and then at him.

Suddenly, he paused in his screaming, peering at me. The room was silent for a second.

'Why are you covered in paint?!' Kai loudly demands. He's confused.

I begin by telling him that I am really lucky, because I have the best job in the world.

'I'm a really lucky adult. I've got the best job in the world. Do you know what the best job in the world is? I'm a Play Therapist and I get to play with toys and do art all day.'

'You're a fucking grown up! Grown-ups don't have toys! You fucking weirdo!'.

I don't flinch. It's okay, I've been called worse. I was expecting him to call me a Peado (he seems that sort of child); being called Weirdo is far less offensive. *I can deal with that and at least he isn't trying to bite me,* I think to myself.

Eventually he calms down, and I ask him would he like to come and have a look at my toys. I've succeeded in calming him and rousing his curiosity[8]. He's never heard of an adult who has toys before. The teachers let him go, he grabs my hand and skips down the corridor with me. I've just picked up my next referral.

Later that day, I had a discussion with his teacher and she told me that the day before, Kai had had contact with his birth father. He is new in the school and geographical area. The school only knows that he was put into foster care aged three, after being found in a flat full of drugged up people. Apparently he was found by a police officer during a drugs raid. It was the middle of winter, and the poor little mite was sitting on a concrete floor, naked and eating frozen chicken nuggets. I already know I'll be working with Kai for a long time.

---

[8] Another brilliant strategy for calming kids (or adults actually) is to help them feel curious about something. It's physically impossible to be curious and anxious at the same time, the brain just can't work both processes simultaneously.

13
Not yet Fernando

I had trained in therapy and entered this shocking world of child abuse and neglect, and for years, I was totally absorbed in my work. Fernando would occasionally mention that we should think about having a baby. I kept smiling and nodding, saying soon, but I wasn't quite ready. Like I said, the job had changed me. I was too busy working my heart out for these kids. As well as working full time as a therapist, I was also working part-time as an advocate for kids in care. I was working 50 hours a week, some weeks more. I was on a crusade, and at the time that felt more important than bringing my own child into the world. There were so many who needed saving. I couldn't disappear into a cloud of baby bliss myself, it just felt too selfish.

In both my jobs, I spent my working life fighting for these kids, fighting the system, fighting labels like 'Manipulative, aggressive, has behavioural problems', 'Child significantly under attainment target: probable learning disorder', 'Child displays Oppositional Defiance Disorder', 'Child steals food, does not understand boundaries', 'Child has assaulted teacher.'.

Read that again and think about those words.

Manipulative… Aggressive…. Stupid… Defiant… Steals… Violent….

I think I can say, hand on heart, that every single child I have ever worked with described in these ways has been the victim of something done to them by an adult, usually the one supposedly looking after them.

Instead of having my own kids, I was busy standing up for these children, giving context to hastily made judgements. I argued with parents, social workers, judges, foster carers, doctors, schools, teachers, anyone I had to, to help these children be understood.

Sometimes I was listened to, and I like to believe that these children benefited a little bit as a result.

All this time I had been working with extremely vulnerable children and young people. I worked with the resulting issues and behaviours and I helped pick up the pieces. I didn't have much experience of children from safe, secure homes that had been loved and cared for properly and hadn't been traumatised.

But I didn't know it at the time. I didn't know that no child of mine would ever be damaged in this way, not whilst I had a breath in my body. I just saw myself as another adult who could damage a child.

Stupid me.

Children are so precious, it frightened me how easy it was to ruin their whole lives by fucking up those few early years. I worked myself stupid in a crusade to help them. I didn't have time to even think about having my own. How could I, in good faith, bring a child into this awful world? When so many other kids needed me? I buried the turmoil in work. Whilst I loved my job, looking back, I think it was breaking my heart a little bit every day. It was, without a doubt, putting me off having my own child. My resolve to not have children seemed to be secretly strengthening, whilst Fernando really wanted to try; I loved him and I wanted to make him happy. I think it's a testament to how much I love him that even though I was terrified, even though I'd been put off all these years, that I agreed we would try in a year's time.

I won't pretend that that year didn't feel very short. Especially after an encounter with a Scary. I remember around this time I was in the supermarket Gossip & Groceries, piling my shopping onto the conveyor belt and waiting to pay. I noticed there was a little girl - she couldn't have been older than two years old, if she was even two – hovering on her own by the pick and mix sweets. I watched her as her little fingers snuck under the plastic lid.

'Indigo!!!!???!!!!' screeched a posh voice. 'You are a vegetarian!!!! Those contain bits of animals!!!!!! Gelatine!!! Uch! Gross!'

She snatched at Indigo's little hand and marched off leaving Indigo looking confused. There was quite a queue to pay, so I was there a while. I watched little Indigo as she wrestled internally. Did the poor little thing even know what the word gelatine meant? Shouldn't her mother have been explaining kindly to her? Whenever I see a young child on their own, I feel a responsibility towards them. I experience a little spike of anxiety that something bad is going to happen to them. It happens all the time, when I see little ones walking right on the edge of the pavement, or a child on their own in a supermarket. Nine times out of ten all is good, and a responsible adult quickly catches up with their child but regularly and usually with raised eyebrows, I ask people pointedly,

'Is this your child…?'

I think it comes with the job. I think people genuinely don't realise what can happen to children if you neglect them.

Poor Indigo had been left by the offensive pick and mix sweets as her mum marched away to the other end of Gossip & Groceries. It seemed like all she cared about was making sure that everyone in the vicinity knew about her vegetarianism, not that her poor kid was confused and had been left on her own. Anyone could have picked her up and made off with her. Honestly… fucking Scarys!

I wasn't in a hurry to join the parenting world, especially not if it was going to be like that.

Soon I would be coming up to 30, so it was probably time. I was very laid back about it though, because I didn't know then how fleeting and precious my fertility would be.

14
Jamie was different

At work, my heart kept hurting by the stories of these children, I worked my arse off for them. Even when I thought I had heard it all, I'd always be gobsmacked again by a different kind of awful story. Childhood trauma is like that you see; you've never heard it all.

But every now and then, a kid would be referred to me, and there didn't seem to be a reason why they were going off the rails. I was starting to put two and two together. During those two years I met a few children and young people who had been, I think, babies born to mothers who had gone through postnatal depression.

The penny began to drop for me when I met Jamie and his family, and his situation got me thinking. An accomplished skier and pianist, middle class 14-year-old Jamie had fallen in with a crowd of young people who spent far more time smoking cannabis (and getting through ridiculous amounts of it) than they did being educated when they were at school.

When Jamie arrived for his session I could feel a sort of sadness seeping out of him, filling the therapy room with a need, a lack, a desire for something I didn't understand. He lived in a massive mansion, went on foreign holidays four times a year, had access to what seemed to be unlimited amounts of money that he could use. Yet he was smoking so much cannabis that he couldn't function. Cannabis is not supposed to be addictive, you aren't supposed to be able to get addicted to cannabis, or experience withdrawal symptoms. But I was noticing that a lot of my young people were actually experiencing addiction, if it wasn't physical dependency, it was definitely mental. Maybe it was the strength of the stuff they had access to, I don't know. I was never an expert on the actual substances that my kids were using, just the reasons that they felt the need to block out the world.

When I went through his family history and had meetings with both Mum and Dad (divorced but not particularly messy, no issues that stood out to me), I began to realise that something had happened to this boy in his infancy. His parents couldn't understand why he wasn't happy and achieving academically like his two siblings. Until this point, I didn't really ask about the very early lives of the young people referred to me. Dad kept referring to the marked difference between Jamie and his siblings. I kept seeing a certain look of guilt pass over Mum's face, a mixture of guilt and shame; I decided to probe more into how he was different to his brother and sister. I began to ask about his relationships with his family members and if anything particularly traumatic had happened to him that may not have happened to his siblings.

In my job you need to expect the unexpected, at this point in any conversation I have with a client's parents, social worker or adoptive parents I have to have an extremely open mind and maintain a calm exterior, no matter what shocking things I am told. But this time, Jamie's parents couldn't seem to think of anything that may have affected him, apart from their divorce. Mum was clearly thinking about something else, whilst Dad bulldozed the conversation (I could see why *he* was now single!). I asked if I could speak to them separately, under the guise of asking them something about current contact arrangements. Dad huffed and puffed a bit, but eventually lifted himself out of the chair and went through into the waiting room outside my office. Mum took a deep breath and I assured her that it was okay to talk to me confidentially. She began telling me that her relationship with Jamie in comparison to his siblings was very different and she didn't understand why.

'Right from the very start it was different with Jamie. I didn't feel the same about him as I did with his older brother and then with his younger sister. I had to have an emergency C-section with him. It was awful. I felt so ill after having him and it went on for months and I'm afraid… I'm really scared that I didn't love him properly when he was first born.'

'It sounds like you had a terrible time giving birth to him, I'm not surprised you felt so ill. Do you think you might have had postnatal depression?'

'Yes. Yes, I do. I was so ashamed though I didn't tell anyone how bad I was feeling and now, now I think it's my fault things are so bad with him. I know his father blames me.'

It sounded as though Jamie's mother had indeed experienced postnatal depression. So I started to read up on it, and learned enough that it started raising flags for me in a few other cases too. Jamie and I worked together for about three months. I also had some time with him and his Mum, and it was sad to see the jagged edges in their relationship. As well as the bullish father, who I undoubtedly suspected had something to do with how Jamie was feeling, I wondered how much of these jagged edges had been ripped by the post-natal experiences this woman had suffered fifteen years before.

Usually, at birth, an incredibly strong bond forms between a mother and her offspring. An ancient, instinctive, ethereal ribbon ties them to each other; the bond beginning well before birth as the baby swims inside its mother, tuning in to her voice. Once outside the womb, fresh air hitting them in the face (which must also be a shock), the arms that usually hold them most of the time in the days after, are those of the mother, and the child responds.

71

'Oh yes, Mumsie Dahhling, it's you, I remember your smell, I remember your voice, give us a bit of the good stuff out of that nipple and all will be good.'

This is the child's very first physical and emotional connection to another human being and over the coming months and years, one which will shape all his future relationships. This thing that happens is cross-species, it's not just us humans who do it. We are pack animals; our emotional and social connections to one another are vital for our survival.

But… when this thing doesn't happen properly, it can seriously affect the child's future mental health and their ability to have healthy relationships; sometimes for the rest of their lives. The proper word for the thing, this early important connection is attachment.

Attachment is bigger than just this connection though; as well as the actual bond, this attachment thing is like an invisible piggy bank, where children store information about how other human beings will treat them; now and in the future; they begin to predict human responses, and adapt their behaviour to match these expectations. For example, a child who is left repeatedly screaming when hungry will become conditioned to think;

'There's no point relying on big humans to feed me so I might as well stay quiet,' which translates and is stored in the piggybank as *'Don't ask for help because you won't get any. Other humans do not care. Other humans will not meet your needs. You are not important.'* That child, if they experience that condition enough times, will remain silent. Remember little Tom? That's how the piggy bank of experiences work.

We all have these piggybanks; they are with us our whole lives. The memories and experiences we have of how our adults treated us as children become the blueprints of how we expect people to treat us, and in turn how to respond to them. So, what I'm trying to say is, if the thing doesn't happen, crappy early attachment experiences can lead to lifelong difficulties in having relationships and interacting with other human beings.

I see it in work all the time. The look in these children's faces breaks my heart. Every day of my working life I see children and young people who have been damaged by something, sometimes it's repeatedly shit experiences with crap parents.

I began to realise that a failure in this connection was very possible not because of shit parenting, but because of postnatal depression. Had Jamie's mum not experienced postnatal depression, would his life be different? It seemed the only explanation. She said the first birth had been natural and unproblematic, the third had been a planned C-section after the problems she had had with Jamie's birth. She told me she didn't feel sadness and the anxiety after those births, only with Jamie. I really felt for the woman, but I didn't understand it then, not really. Remember my only understanding of it really was the stories my Nain had told me. Nowhere in my training had we covered it. At all. I only knew from learning from my Nain that years ago, some women ended up in The Mental because of Insanity caused by Childbirth. I knew that The Criminal Mastermind's mother had gone strange after having him (but she was odd before so that didn't really mean anything to me). I knew a lot about Attachment, and I started to make links in my head about this and how kids might get affected by their mother's mental health after childbirth.

These were just thoughts percolating in my mind. I didn't have many kids referred to me like Jamie, just once in a while. Most of my time in work was taken up with the kids who had been neglected, abused, involved in crime, who were drinking a lot, using drugs and that sort of thing. I had a lot of kids like India, Kelly and Ivan, sadly a few who I suspected would end up like John, but not many like Jamie.

I was building a reputation (I feel so bigheaded saying this but it's true) for being able to connect with damaged, traumatised and given-up-on kids... their stories horrifying to hear and their solutions challenging to find. I would sometimes be the only adult they could trust or show their true selves to. I'm very proud of those kids I worked with who flourished, and I was proud of the career I was carving out for myself. I felt I had found my niche.

I was working hard and relaxing from the horrors of my job by playing hard. I dread to think how much money Fernando and I spent on alcohol back then, we were both party animals. We probably spent enough to pay off the rest of our mortgage...ouch.

Eventually I began warming to the idea of having a baby, but this was completely separate to the recent discoveries I was making in work. Postnatal depression wasn't anything to do with me personally. Of course it wasn't! It didn't ever occur to me that I might ever go through anything like that.

As a kid myself I was a total tomboy and I hated dollies. I still feel a bit spooked at those dollies, you know the ones whose eyes close when you tip them backwards? Ew...so creepy.

I've never been that interested in tiny babies either. In fact, let me tell you a secret... I don't really like babies, not until they are a few months old. They remind me of those dollies a bit and I'm always a bit scared of breaking them. They are a bit boring too. Don't judge me.... and please don't tell anyone.

15
It's official - I'm a twat

I'd gone years avoiding listening to anything related to having babies. Back when my first nephew was born, I'd even *accidentally-on-purpose* orchestrated being out of the country.

'I cannot fucking believe that you booked a holiday on purpose for her due date. You are her fucking sister!' Sleepless Beauty said, when she found out.

I know. It's awful isn't it? But my job was so stressful, Hosenose's life was always so dramatic, and we didn't really get on back then. I didn't want to know about labour. I'd spent two agonizing fucking days like some weirdly absent expectant father, absolutely shitting myself when Sleepless Beauty and my other good friend Manykids were in labour for the first time. It was awful, I genuinely thought they were going to die.

So after that, I buried my head in the sand and hummed a tune with my fingers stuck in my ears when anything giving-birth-related was brought up. When Hosenose told me she was pregnant I wanted nothing to do with the process.

'You fucking tool. You are only 19 years old'. I know. What a twat. But after the labours of Manykids and Sleepless Beauty, I really couldn't cope with the whole Birth thing so, head buried deep within my own arse, I booked a holiday on purpose for the week that my sister, Hosenose, was due her first baby. Yes… I did that. I know… it's really bad…I'm such a twat[9].

Then they all started!

A thousand times over, I would rather have been partying on a beach in Thailand, (well past my best before date), than in a soft play area drinking lukewarm coffee, my ear drums

---

[9] Pie, just so you know, you being born was actually one of the best things to ever happen to me. I love being Auntie to you, Loobie and Tiny G.

bursting with the sound of fifty thousand kids all screaming with excitement. I didn't understand.

Didn't my friends realise what they were letting themselves in for??

I shuddered a bit at the Baby Club that my gang were joining, one by one. I spent a fair amount of time in my twenties buying new baby cards, cute outfits, bottles of vodka to celebrate being able to drink again (yes, and I still do that to this day). There are countless pictures of me, the spinster auntie, holding the various new-born offspring of my gang, plastered in make up so you couldn't tell I had a massive hangover. Holding my breath in order not to poison the new-born's tiny little lungs with last night's alcohol-tinged breath.

I congratulated and smiled for them in their happiness. I sympathised with the trials and changes that my friends and family members faced in becoming mothers. If I'm honest, I thought they were exaggerating when they told me how little sleep they lived on, how tough it all was.

It can't be that bad, I thought, because some of them decided to do it again! In the case of Manykids, she did it again, and again, and again, and then again and again as she later added to her family – she is one brave motherfucker[10]. I watched as Manykids continued to populate the world, depriving herself of more and more sleep. As gorgeous as each baby was, it looked a bit to me like a strange form of self-harm.

I secretly wondered if my gang knew that their cute babies and adorable children would eventually turn into these scary teenagers and shuddered at what was to come. I didn't fancy having a couple of gorgeous babies only for them to grow up and to cause mayhem and tell me that they hated me. And they were gorgeous, the babies that is, but the side effects (oh dear, I

---

[10] Sorry Manykids. Love you. You are a great Mum too x

76

think I just said side effects when referring to babies) made me wonder what all the fuss was about. Inwardly I was sad for my mates, for example when they couldn't get a babysitter - I remember this being a bit irritating when I was childless and didn't understand the pure gold of a good babysitter - or when they enviously asked me about my social life.

Whilst I sympathised with them rather disingenuously, I secretly thanked my lucky stars that I still had one. This does not mean I didn't care. All aforementioned offspring of my friends and family love me. I am definitely high in the Favourite Auntie league tables.

16
Over before it began.

That year of freedom came to an end, it was the right time, and as promised I stopped taking my contraceptive pill. Very quickly, I fell pregnant. This chapter doesn't have a happy ending and should probably come with a trigger warning.

Some things are still raw and maybe unprocessed in my mind. I can't allow myself to think very much about what I'm about to tell you because it hurts. I won't edit this chapter once it's written. I can't look at it again, because six months before I became pregnant with Wolfgang, I had a miscarriage. Very quickly I'd fallen pregnant. Fernando was over the moon and I was beginning to smile about it too. I went for a scan at 9 weeks and spent the next three weeks on a roller coaster of emotions. I was elated, scared, happy and worried all at the same time, smiling to myself at our secret. Although at first I'd been reluctant to have a baby, now I had one, I really wanted her.

Then at my 12-week scan, they told me that the foetus had died. My baby was dead. The dream was over, before it had begun. I didn't tell anyone but I kind of thought I deserved it. Because I hadn't wanted it enough.

I was given some tablets and booked into the hospital to pass the baby. It was one of the worst days of my life... I lay in a side room on a Labour ward all day. I didn't know what I was supposed to do. Did I lie on the bed? Apart from pain, I wasn't ill. Strangely I agonised over sitting on the bed, because I didn't need it, I didn't want to make a mess of it.

On my own, a random nurse would pop in every few hours to see if 'anything had happened yet?'. Fernando had to work and couldn't be with me. I have never felt so utterly broken, useless and alone.

I was so ashamed, and convinced that if only I had been more excited and more grateful, that maybe this baby would have survived. It was only when my baby had died that I realised how much I wanted her. I don't know why but I've always thought of that baby as a her. Somewhere on the ward, someone kept playing the song '*Songbird*' by Ella Fitzgerald. I must've heard it 15 times that day.

I didn't pass anything at all. Eventually I was discharged. And that was that. My next period was awfully heavy but then that was no different for me. I sat on the toilet at home a couple of days later, crying my eyes out. Was it bits of my poor baby or was it just a normal period? I guess I will never know. Pain and huge amounts of bleeding were not unusual for me anyway. Every period in those days was extremely heavy.

Even now, ten years later, I can't listen to that song. I guess someone on that ward was playing it to their new-born, and it's a song that brings joy to them. It takes me to a place of horror.

Endometriwhatsit?

Before I fell pregnant the first time, I had been under investigation by the gynaecologist. Stupid me, I didn't realise that periods are not supposed to be so painful that you can't sit on a hard surface for several days every month. I didn't realise that not everyone has such heavy periods that they have to wear two sanitary pads and a tampon at the same time, just to stop anything leaking. I though everyone was like this and I was just a wimp.

It got worse in my early 20s. I remember the first time I thought things weren't right. Fernando and I were on a night out and I'd had a lot to drink. I should have been pretty anesthetised by the amount of alcohol I'd consumed. I was chatting to a lady that I knew who was sitting on a low bar stool. She invited me to join her and sit down. I couldn't. I literally couldn't bend myself down to sit on the stool, because when I tried to, the pain in my pelvis area was horrific.

The following month the same thing happened again, but instead of resting and looking after myself, I went out drinking again, because I'm clever like that. A few hours later when all the pubs were shut and we were walking home, I collapsed. I was pissed out of my mind but also had this pain like never before. Fernando carried me home and called an ambulance.

In the hospital they gave me painkillers and put me on a drip for the rest of the weekend. Because I had drunk so much there was a lot of tutting and I don't think I was taken very seriously. I wasn't examined at all, and was sent home with some medication for something called Pelvic Inflammatory Disease and a stern warning not to drink so much, which studiously I decided to ignore. Pelvic Inflammatory Disease is a sexually transmitted infection.

I DID NOT have a fucking STI.

I had a disease called Endometriosis, but I didn't know it at the time. It took years for me to get over the shame and receive a proper diagnosis.

I DID NOT have a fucking STI.

Two things didn't help with the shame of thinking I had a sexually transmitted infection.

I DID NOT have a fucking STI.

The first was that my Nain (the mental health nurse and a very strong influence on me), who had died earlier that year, had always instilled in me that I should stay away from boys.
'Stay away from boys or you will have women's problems'

Was what she literally said to me when I was about 13 years old, and it had stuck with me. I hadn't stayed away from the boys, and now I apparently had an STI. I was grieving badly for her, she had died less than a year before this happened, so she was on my mind a lot. I felt like I had let her down.

But I DID NOT have a fucking STI.

Secondly, my boss at the time taught sexual health in schools. So explaining why I had had to take a few days off because of excruciating pelvic pain that the hospital had fobbed off as Pelvic Inflammatory Disease was extremely embarrassing. She was lovely about it and I'm still in touch with her, and I still want her to know that…

I DID NOT have a fucking STI.

Talking about how bosses deal with diseases like endometriosis, I should probably tell you about a delightful little man who we shall call Moonface. Moonface was part of the reason I left my last employed job and decided to go self-employed. Apart from the fact that Moonface was a complete bell-end, it was hard to manage things like back to work interviews and the hassle of being off work ill too much (anyone who works in a public funded authority will probably shudder at the words Bradford Points). In 2016, when I would become my own boss, it would be much easier to take time off because of the pain endometriosis caused me, and work around it. I couldn't afford not to work, and the stress of Moonface and the other bullshit was making me sicker.

Everything about that vile little man was a sort of beige colour. His hair, his skin, his clothes, and his personality. If he were an animal, I think he would be a cream-coloured micro pig. How the hell Moonface had got a job as a manager I don't know, I swear, he couldn't find his own arse using both hands. He was one of these shouty let's-empower-everyone kind of people. He protested a lot about how he believed in equality whilst really he was, quite clearly, a thinly-veiled male-chauvinist twat.

The endometriosis was so bad at this point, I ended up having to take a day or two off work every month. I did ask if I could work from home on those days, but Moonface refused, on the grounds that '*all the* other *girls come in during their time of month*'.

The dance of me being off sick and Moonface conducting my back to work interviews followed my absences every month. Every time he would write 'Period Pain' as my reason for being off work. He probably couldn't spell endometriosis.

He really was thick as shit.

It became clear that he fucking hated me. I can see now that as I became more skilled and experienced, the fact that I could run rings around him must've been very uncomfortable for the poor simpleton.

I'm pretty sure he hated me because I ran rings around him. To be fair, you only had to be awake to run rings round the bloody fool. I reckon my two-year-old cockapoo would have done a better job than him. He was a big fan of using words that he didn't know the meaning of. Corporate speak was becoming popular in our workplace. I find corporate speak hideously cringey. Especially when it is used by someone trying to look more intelligent and important than they actually are. After twenty years working in public funded organisations I'd heard it all, believe me. If you ask me to 'think outside the box', or to put my 'blue sky thinking hat' on, or tell me that you will get back to me by the 'close of play', to me, you have immediately lost any scrap of professional credibility you may have had. I might be smiling, but know this, inside I'm judging.

Moonface had clocked on to the fact that managers were using these phrases and started himself, in the silly hope that he would sound more like he had the slightest fucking clue what he was doing. The day he asked me to 'populate the spreadsheet', something inside me snapped like an overstretched elastic band. I couldn't take any more of working with this idiot, and the day after I resigned.

Moonface was one of the reasons I eventually got some sort of diagnosis actually, so maybe the halfwit did help me in some way. Because he kept insisting on me getting a doctor's note to explain my time off. I found out later that I didn't technically need a doctor's note for the short amount of time I was having off, but obviously he wanted to make my life difficult.

Sick of all this, I had finally gotten up the guts to speak to the doctor about it again. Other than heavy and very painful periods, something else strange was happening to me every month. Just before my period, for three days, my right arm would hurt really badly. Then as soon as I came on my period the pain in my arm would stop. It radiated down from my shoulder and was so bad that it would take my breath away. The pain was like a migraine or a tooth abscess but in my shoulder. It would be twelve years before they realised that I had Endometriosis that was so bad that it had infiltrated my liver and diaphragm, and that this was affecting a nerve causing the pain in my shoulder. Several doctors fobbed me off, sent me to shoulder specialists, did MRIs on my shoulder, sent me to physio and even questioned my mental health, but there was nothing wrong with my actual bloody shoulder.

Eventually after years of fighting with specialists, I was referred to a new one, who miraculously had just been to a conference about something called Diaphragmatic Endometriosis. It turned out I had it. Twelve years after my first symptoms, I would finally have a 6-hour surgery with this surgeon, during which they would take out a piece of my liver and cut the disease out of my diaphragm. The pain in my shoulder would disappear, but for now it was excruciating.

Apart from my shoulder and my pelvis, a lot of other things were hurting too. It was beginning to hurt to wee, and having sex was often out of the question. My bowels were so bad that some days there would be teeth marks on the toilet door, I was that constipated. Other days the diarrhoea would be so bad I would be stuck on the toilet for hours. The painful explosions were sometimes so bad that Fernando asked me if I wanted him to attach a seatbelt to the toilet, the twat! Fernando and I have a deal. We don't do pity. We don't do sympathy.

In regard to my endometriosis, he does me a favour and takes the piss mercilessly. He tells me I'm milking it, that I'm attention-seeking and that endometriosis can't possibly be worse than a kick in the balls.

'You're bloody lucky you don't have testicles. You're lucky that you don't have balls, coz I'm telling you now, a kick in the balls is ten times worse than this little problem you've got. I'm telling you.'

This way, I can fight back, I can grin and take the piss back, threaten to kick him in the balls and not feel ashamed of the times he has literally had to help me off the toilet, clean up blood stains from when I have haemorrhaged, push me in wheelchairs, accompany me to hundreds of hospital appointments, had to abstain from intimacy for months at a time and all the loveliness that comes with this disease. If he felt sorry for me, I think I would have given up by now.

After Wolfgang was born, this shitty disease got a whole lot worse. Endometriosis affects 1 in 10 women, apparently. It's an awful disease but I think because it doesn't actually kill you, and probably because it only affects women, it's not been taken that seriously in the medical world. To put it into perspective, in the medical research world, erectile dysfuckingfunction has attracted five times more funding than research into endometriosis. There seems to be a huge gender bias in what the medical community is interested in funding. Before my first pregnancy, the butcher, I mean gynaecologist at my local hospital, wanted to operate and give me a full hysterectomy.

Would a surgeon remove a man's balls to see if it cured pain in his shoulder…? I don't fucking think so!

Thankfully I had the support of a local advocacy group for women's health conditions. I learnt through them that a hysterectomy would not cure me. I can't thank them enough, and just as a lump arises in my throat when I think of what I owe them, a lump of any profits made from this book will be heading their way for sure. They literally saved my womb, and by advocating on my behalf they got me referred to a specialist gynaecologist who said I didn't have to have a hysterectomy yet. Without the support of FTWW Fair Treatment for the Women of Wales, my son, Wolfgang, would not exist.

17
Trying Again

After the miscarriage, my gynaecology referral was put on hold when we told them we were trying for a baby again. But in truth I kept taking my pill, scared of what had happened, scared of what was to come. At this point, I still didn't know that endometriosis could stop me from even having a baby, I'd only just had a diagnosis and didn't know much about the disease. Nobody knew how bad the disease would become. I wouldn't find out until way after Wolfgang was born. Getting pregnant[11] used to be encouraged by doctors as a cure for endometriosis. Some still recommend it! Now we know that while the symptoms do go away while you are pregnant, as soon as your body returns to pre-pregnancy hormone levels, endometriosis returns with a vengeance. For some women like me, it comes back even worse.

After the trauma of the miscarriage Fernando and I agreed to have one more summer of holidays before we tried again. In our late twenties we felt like pensioners in Ibiza, but we had a ball nonetheless. Sitting together outside Café del Mar watching the sun going down to some chilled dance music is a memory I'll never forget.

When we returned from Ibiza, hungover to hell and feeling like we needed a holiday, I took a deep breath and didn't order my repeat prescription of birth control pills. (I thought that was going to sound more dramatic than it did.)

A month later, we recklessly booked another holiday last minute to Egypt. Two weeks of all-inclusive fun. Egypt was having a heatwave that summer. Egypt is bloody hot anyway,

---

[11] Pregnancy does not cure Endometriosis, although some doctors without recent training in gynaecological diseases will still say this. Sigh.

but the summer we went it was ridiculous. Reeling from the miscarriage and the fact I was on holiday without my trusty pill packet I booked us on to every excursion and adventure possible, to take my mind off it.

It was on one of these excursions into the desert that we must have picked up food poisoning. Fighting for the bathroom, Fernando and I spent the middle weekend of the holiday in our thankfully (phew!) air-conditioned room. Two days of non-stop vomiting and diarrhoea, it was the only holiday where I have come home skinnier than when I left. The smell that must have come from that room... I seem to remember I actually shat in the bath I was so desperate, whilst Fernando was doubled over on the toilet. I'm not sure if this is accurate or not, I'll have to ask him.

Anyway, two days later, we were much better and back out on the razz. Apart from those awful two days I really enjoyed that holiday. Fernando however, has vowed to never set foot in Egypt again.

A week after I arrived home, I felt the familiar queasiness and breast tenderness.

I was pregnant again.

19
A Pregnant Idiot

Apt as I was back then, after a traumatic experience, instead of talking about it, I wiped my previous miscarriage from my mind (Yes, I'm a therapist. You have to do what I say, not what I do). Nothing was going to happen to this baby.

Everything was going to be perfect.

I used to consider myself to be a fairly intelligent person. Wow, that sounds an even more arrogant statement written down, than it did in my head, but bear with me... because at the same time I also have a secret fear that I'm wrong, and that really I've greatly overestimated my level of intelligence. I'm scared that in real life I am thick as shit. This is the reason I point blank refuse to do an IQ test. Just in case it comes back with an awful score. Because I suspect it might. I think it might. My ego would never, ever survive that.

If there was a test to measure the intelligence of pregnant women on the topic of giving birth, I would have scored a minus 50. I was astoundingly naïve about the upcoming birth. I can't quite believe how daft I was. Now I know it was in response to what had happened with my previous pregnancy. Looking back at my pregnant days, I imagine myself as a fat little fairy, floating about, enjoying the spoiling and consideration reserved solely for the pregnant. I imagine that fat little fairy (in a glittery tutu for some reason) introducing herself.

'Hello there. I'm a pregnant. I'm also an idiot! I'm going to have a water birth, you know!'

I didn't have a fucking water birth.

My pregnancy flew by. I had a few complications but nothing really bad. A couple of little scares, a couple of visits to the hospital to be monitored because Wolfgang was having a lazy day and not moving. Although scary, these events only happened twice, I think. I also had this painful condition called Symphysis Pubis Dysfunction (SPD) which is something to do with the ligaments loosening too much in your pelvis. The ligaments, bless them, are trying to prepare you for labour by becoming more flexible, but for me and up to 1 in 5 pregnant women, too much of a particular hormone is released, and cause the ligaments become too flexible. Thankfully mine wasn't all that bad, I had a strange walk (even stranger than the normal pregnant waddle) and had to wear a kind of weightlifting belt; I was lucky, for some women in severe cases… I'm shaking like a shitting dog thinking about the horror of this… the pelvis can actually split…

In case you haven't guessed yet, Wolfgang's birth went badly. Very badly. I think the awful birth was a huge contributing factor to me developing postnatal depression. I'd spent such a long time choosing the first perfect babygrow, my relaxing music and that stupid hummingbird-patterned dressing gown, which still hangs on the back of the bathroom door as a relic of my survival. I even had a gel manicure and a sodding luxury pedicure a few days before. Preparing myself for childbirth with beautiful silver talons. Sitting here shaking my head writing this… I really would not even consider the possibility that things would not go perfectly to plan. A close friend of mine I call The Enforcer (loyal, gorgeous, a bit scary at times, and is the person I would want standing behind me if I was ever brave enough to have a fight) had had a child eighteen months previously. She is six years younger than me, and I've always felt quite maternal towards her.

She had a horrific time giving birth to my god-daughter. But, instead of opening my eyes to what could go wrong, I blocked out her experience and naively decided that that was not going to happen to me. What a bell-end I am!

I had been warmly encouraged by the midwife (who was obviously as stupid as I was) to choose lovely birthing plans like opting for a water birth, using gas and air only, Fernando massaging me with soothing essential oils. Gloriously calm music, hell, maybe I'd even give some whale music a go. I studiously wrote it all in my birthing plan, perfectly confident that this was exactly what was going to happen.

Birthing plan? I laugh now, with the same knowing twinkle in my eye, that look that mothers have, and mothers-to-be have not. It's probably a slight glaze of sleeplessness, disenchantment, guilt, and overwhelming love. A complex mix, eh? My advice about birthing plans would be to plan for the worst and hope for the best. Or keep it for emergency toilet paper for reasons that will become clear.

Oh yes, and the hilarity of this…. I had decided that there was no way I was going to have a caesarean so put that completely out of my mind. Guess what? I had an emergency caesarean section… which completely traumatised me. And not a drop of hippy oil or a single ditty sung from one supportive whale.

20
Swimming with Hippos

There are a lot of saccharine assumptions about being pregnant. Cravings, nesting, enjoying the transformation of your body, blah blah blah. Apparently some magic thing happens where you want to clean everything and prepare your house for the big day and it's called Nesting. I didn't get this. My house continued (and continues to this day) to be a chaotic, passably clean, relaxed, but quite an untidy space.

When I was pregnant, I remember dreamily wondering if I would start eating coal or munching on bath sponges. I didn't really have cravings as such, but I ate my way through enough custard creams to keep a custard cream factory open for a few weeks. But I think that was just greed. Perhaps I wouldn't be this fat, years later if I had opted for bath sponges. So there's a piece of advice... actually shit, no. I better not. Don't eat bath sponges.

As mine and Sleepless Beauty's bellies grew, she suggested we went to a ~~swimming for hippos~~ antenatal aquafit class. The humourless and scary midwife on the side of the pool barked orders at us. I did my best not to drown, grumbling like a petulant child that I would rather drink piss than be there. Being so short, I reckon I swallowed so much water, attempting these crazy moves, that I probably did drink a bellyful of piss. This evening was when I first met Pubwatch and Chickenkicker, both of them first time mothers like me.

Sleepless Beauty was busy trying to pretend she wasn't with me as I cheerfully made an idiot of myself, loudly whinging and busy trying not to drown. Suddenly, this polyester-mix-swimwear-clad angel, with an obviously pregnant belly, dive - bombed her way into the middle of us.

'Room for a little one!?' she yelled as she gloriously soared through the air, a vision of navy blue and defiance. The midwife looked on in disgust as she splashed into the middle of our group.

I was laughing so much I gulped a mouthful of water down, choked and I added my own bit of urine to the lovely mix that I already suspected was in the pool. (The midwife's face was a picture, even more so a few weeks later when Pubwatch was quite confrontational with her about the wisdom of eating copious amounts of scones during a discussion about pregnancy and weight control. The midwife took the conversation very seriously, whilst Pubwatch was quite clearly taking the piss. It was hilarious.)

Later, in the shower after that first class, I was still sniggering to myself about Pubwatch's entrance, when this refreshingly hippy-looking lady stood next to me in the communal shower area. I hadn't seen her before and I noticed she had really cool hair which was shaved on one side. Her protruding belly and wet hair suggested she had been in hippo swimming class too. She was much taller than me so was probably rocking it in the deep end.

She leaned her gracious self down to my ear level (I think I was a Shetland Pony in a previous life, whilst she was more like a thoroughbred) and out of the blue, whispered into my ear.

'Um, do you think I will have to take my piercing out from you know, *down there*, to uh you know, have the baby?'

Spitting out shampoo I tried to think of a reply. I knew a seriously intimate thing about this woman and I didn't even know her name. Looking back, I'm not even sure what my reply was, but I'm pretty certain I fell in love with both Pubwatch and Chickenkicker a bit that night. I felt a connection to these two wonderful women for their differences and sense of humour.

93

I never asked if Chickenkicker had taken her piercing out. Did you pal?

In case you are wondering, Pubwatch is called that because she has an horrific temper. She is the loveliest person and I still struggle to believe it, but before we met she used to go out and get banned from the local pubs for fighting. These days she's a home-schooling mum and is very, very respectable 90% of the time, but I reckon if a judging Scary got too close to her she would deck them. I love Pubwatch, and her lovely sister, The Doula, who owns the best cake shop and café around. The Doula as we called her, prefers dogs to kids, but came to our meet ups when our babies were small and supported Pubwatch and the rest of us with our struggles, fair play to her, what a star. When they both turned up to something, you knew your sides would soon be splitting, and your anxiety levels would plummet. And the cakes….oooh the cakes…. The Doula used to bring samples for us to try. Mmmm.

So while Pubwatch had moved up the social ladder, Chickenkicker on the other hand, used to be respectable but now isn't really (soz Chickenkicker). She used to have a high up job in the Police, and although she had left her job by the time she met me, Pubwatch and Sleepless Beauty, we definitely dragged her down into the gutter. The first Christmas we met up for our yearly piss up, she was dressed to the nines. Apart from her footwear. Head to ankle she was glammed up to the nines, but on her feet she wore the biggest pair of fluffy chicken feet slippers.

I have no idea why she does this.

She turned up in a restaurant another Christmas do dressed in a full-size Dalek costume. I shit you not, this is absolutely true... We were all sitting at the table wondering where she was when this full-size bloody Dalek slowly walks towards us, popped it's head off and shouts 'Surprise!' in hysterical giggles.

We hadn't planned fancy dress or anything, she just thinks these stunts are hilarious. I've just had a thought – I wonder if Chickenkicker's postnatal madness came out in her *accessories*? Hmmm. I never thought of that!

Chickenkicker, Pubwatch and I bonded at Swimming for Hippos and stayed in touch. We would go on to form a club, an exhausted band of misfits, Sleepless Beauty, Chickenkicker, Pubwatch, me and a select few beautiful, lovely women (you know who you are ladies); the Scrummies. Basically, membership would be open to anyone struggling a bit with a new baby, who could tolerate a lot of swearing and who didn't appear to be a twat.

21

Meep Meep!

My bump was lovely and petite until I was 38 weeks pregnant. However, in week 39 I swelled up like a balloon. I reckon I must have looked like a child's drawing of a spider with four legs. I couldn't be growing so big because of custard cream calories because I'm convinced I must have been burning calories off as quickly as I was eating them, constantly running back and forth to the toilet. I was like fucking Roadrunner.

Sit down. Eat Custard Cream.

Niawwww up the stairs.

Pee. Flush.

Sit down. Eat Custard Cream.

Niawwwww up the stairs.

Pee. Flush.

Meep Meep.

You get the idea.

About a week before the due date, I remember that I was so tired and fed up of this constant need to wee that I considered 1) not drinking anything so I would get a few hours' peace or 2) just pissing where I was. I was probably already stinking from the few drips that dribbled out every time anyway. But I didn't. Not drinking was probably very bad for the baby, and I thought I smelled bad enough already. So Roadrunner continued visiting the toilet for another week.

Apart from eating custard creams and weeing (probably at the same time), I don't really remember anything else from that week.

The Best Day of my Fucking Life

22

I appear to have procrastinated my way all the way to this chapter before finally, actually, telling you the nitty gritty details of my birth story. I'm still nervous about telling it. Okay, so a deep breath for me. I must remember…this is a shared experience; millions of women experience it.

My due date arrived and so did the midwife – thankfully not the miserable one from Swimming for Hippos. She smiled gently and donned her blue rubber gloves. I lay back on our freshly laundered bed. She then conducted what they call a sweep. To me, a sweep implies a gentle swooshing motion. She said it might feel a bit uncomfortable. I grinned at her in a sort of smug and cheerful way.

'Bring it on… I'm rather brave you know!'

But I was bloody scared, and I felt like a right sissy when I cried out. It was not a bit uncomfortable. It was a very painful, if well-intentioned, invasion of my nether regions. A sweep does not imply a latex covered finger ramming into your most private parts. Ouch. It didn't even work.

Two days later, because I'm a fucking idiot[12], I decided to try and get things moving by helping Hosenose move back home, (she'd had to move to a different house for a few months after the flood so it could all be re-plastered and whatnot). Hosenose wholeheartedly disapproved of my decision and looked on in horror as I determinedly began carrying boxes into her house.

Yeah, that did the trick… I started having contractions in the middle of that night. Apparently they were just little ones but I already thought I was dying. After a panicked phone call from Fernando, Hosenose and Uncle Knobhead came round

[12] Uhhh, yeah. Don't try this at home folks.

very early in the morning looking all dishevelled, like you do when you've moved house the previous day.

She was wearing Uncle Knobhead's underpants and trousers, which I would have found hilarious in normal circumstances... but I could barely crack a smile. She, however, seemed very relaxed for someone whose sister was clearly dying in front of her eyes. She knew. She bloody knew it was going to get a hundred times worse.

Later that day we dutifully went to hospital. I buckled myself into the passenger seat of the truck. As we rumbled along my mind was whirring.

This is it, I'm in fucking agony, the baby will be here in half an hour.

I wonder if we will even get to hospital? Will I have to give birth on the side of the motorway?

Will we be in the paper? Shit, how is Fernando going to cut the cord? Could he use his car key?

Oh my god I've weed a bit again...thank god it's got leather seats.

My thoughts were spiralling into madness. My head span with planning to give birth on the motorway. Then, as we pulled into the hospital car park, it occurred to me what a warrior I was, a proper hero. I'd waited this long before going to hospital. And we got there without giving birth on the motorway. I waddled on to the maternity ward.

I was immediately examined. Then with a smile from the midwives I was sent home and told to take some paracetamol. Fucking paracetamol! I was told to come back when the contractions were much worse and much more frequent. The plan was for me to attend one of the water birth facilities. I was stunned, severely pissed off, and felt like some sort of fobbed-off drama queen. Clearly I was dying and the hospital was sending me home, instead of saving me. So I went home. The bastards! Then I remembered their words, as we impotently trundled home... the contractions were going to get much worse!

All day I rocked and I moaned and I bounced. I had one of those inflatable yoga ball things. I must have bounced up and down, up and down, like a deranged kangaroo on that fucking ball, I don't know... um... a hundred thousand times. I'm pretty sure I did some damage to the foundations of our house with all that bouncing as my fat arse repeatedly pounded it into the living room floor.

Sleep was out of the question because the pain was awful. At 3am I remember manically bouncing away, watching repeats of a telesales show about a revolutionary new steam mop, (it must have worked, because I ended up buying one a few weeks later). Up and down I went, trying to be engrossed in the steam-mop show, because stopping to reach for the remote control was just too much. I bounced and bounced and bounced... shooting the occasional scathing glance of hatred at the ceiling, in Fernando's direction. He who was sleeping like a smug, carefree, lethargic pig, up in our bedroom.

When the lethargic pig woke up, the contractions had slowed down a bit, with less intensity. They were still there but I was coping.

A few hours later, *bang!* The contractions had become unbearable, and off we trundled back to the hospital...

We got there and found out all three of the water birth facilities were full. Fucking full. All three. I distinctly remember the midwife laughing at the notion that all three facilities would be full when I queried this possibility. She said it had never been a problem before. But in my mind, I was promised a fucking water birth!

I ended up in the midwife-led unit. I was the only one there, probably because every other fucker in the world was having a water birth. The bastards.

The midwife-led unit was a cross between a ghostly soft play area and minimalist's living room. I rocked, moaned, whinged and dutifully tracked each of my contractions on my highly complicated App that I had downloaded especially. I was under the care of Alison. Alison had the most annoying voice I've ever heard. She also clapped like sea lion at regular intervals whilst exclaiming about how clever I apparently was. She was the campest woman I have ever met. She spoke about us in the third person, which was very disconcerting.

'Oooooh, how clever is Mummy? You are doing really well, Mummy! Alison is right here with you! Don't you worry now, Mummy!'

Clap! Clap! Fucking clap!

Alison sent Fernando home…. **for a rest**. Through my teeth (gritted to the point that I don't know how I stopped myself from scathingly replying.

'Oooh dear. Didn't poor little Lethargic Pig get enough sleep last night? Is it tiring seeing Mummy being so fucking clever?')

I seethed at his back as he walked away from me through the double doors. I imagined him clicking his heels like Dick Van fucking Dyke down the corridor and all the way out of the hospital. To be fair he probably wasn't, but in case you haven't guessed, I didn't like him very much at that point.

I was alone for what I think was about two hours. Then something happened. All I remember is an almighty flash of pain. We still don't know what it was, but when Alison finally returned, I was passed out on the squashy foam thing I was rolling on. Everything was NOT all-fucking-right with Mummy.

I don't really remember this but I had managed to ring Dick Van Dyke, screaming at him to come back. Now those who know me well would assume I was just enjoying the gas and air too much and was off my face, but I wasn't, whatever had happened had been so bad that I lost consciousness. I can just about remember trying to focus my eyes to make the phone call before the phone itself and the gas and air pump slipped out of my reach.

Then everything was black until the slow, mad voice of Alison invaded what peace there was to be found in unconsciousness.

'Hi, so how's our Mummy doing? You okay, are you darling? You're doing so well, such a clever Mummy!'

'Oh, hi Alison! Yes thank you, I'm tippity fucking top!'

Clap, clap fucking clap!

I don't actually know if I said anything in reply, but that's what she deserved for asking such a stupid question. Idiotic cow.

They - I don't know who they were, I was just told *they* had decided to move me from the midwife-led unit to the delivery ward. Because there was only me on the unit, the hospital decided that having only one midwife to one mother was poor value for their cash. Alison actually told me this and seemed to expect me to sympathise at the hassle it was causing her, whilst we still hadn't covered the fact that she had found me unconscious. Alison was studiously ignoring the fact.

Afterwards I realised that this might have something to do with the fact that she left me on my own for so long, perhaps she wasn't meant to? I still don't know.

Whatever. Alison could go and fuck herself. Everything had gone to shit. Breaks between contractions had vanished. I seemed to be having what felt like one constant contraction, but apparently, I was *failing to progress*[13].

---

[13] At this point I would like to point out what an awful label/diagnosis that is. The blame I put on myself for failing was horrendous, and probably contributed to my mental state after the birth.

The hospital then decided to put a drip in my arm to induce the birth. Ironically this caused my useless but excruciating contractions to come more extremely. Hours of this agony passed, I moved from screaming to silence and apparently, I was a bit delirious at times.

Eventually a doctor (apparently with more than half a brain this time) examined me and it was decided that somehow, my opened cervix had re-closed. The doctor emerged from between my bestirruped legs, covered in blood up to the elbows. He was very angry.

'Who the hell said this woman was 8 cm?!' he roared. All hell broke loose.

My body had been trying to deliver my son against a closed cervix. I remember them slipping a strange kind of clip into me, attached to the baby's head to monitor him. And that came out covered in blood too and I remember panicking. I thought they had hurt him, maybe even killed him.

He is probably dead. And it's all my fault.

Thankfully, my boy, however, was very much alive and kicking but he was in distress and needed to come out. Fear doesn't come close to describing it, I was at the same time in screaming agony and completely numb. I began to feel detached from it all, as if I was watching what was going on from far, far away. Noises became muffled. I had withdrawn completely into myself. Those who know me know. Like a toddler, if you can't hear me, there's probably trouble.

Withdrawing or disassociating in the way that I was doing, is a classic sign that a person is unconsciously trying to prevent themselves becoming traumatized. It's when the trauma has been too much and the body and brain can't take anymore. Pretty cool our brains are, eh? Obviously I wasn't processing that at the time.

I had been in a state of extreme pain and torturously slow, unrelenting anxiety for two days, and then as the doctor emerged from my 'down there' covered in blood, everything seemed to speed up, as if it was happening in fast forward.

The angry doctor was shouting at other people in the room, although I don't have any recollection of who they were.

My next memory is of an anaesthetist, who had arrived to give me an epidural (long gone was the protestation that *I* was never having an epidural). He asked me did I have any questions. I did. I'm proud to say that my sense of humour hadn't deserted me, even at my lowest, most vulnerable state.

'Yes actually, I do have a question,' I replied. 'Could you try your best not to fuck this up please? I could do with being able to walk again.'

'Of course I will make sure I do the best job that I can Mrs Lunatic…' He was clearly shocked, and not very amused. My desperate attempt at humour had failed.

He sort of fake-smiled and got on with what could be described as separating the two halves of my body. I heard the words 'emergency section' and a set of scrubs was chucked at my husband.

Caesarean Section… two words which produced in me a fear so great, I had not allowed it to crystalize into any sort of potential or possibility….

Apparently, up to one in five women develops mental health problems during pregnancy or in the first year after childbirth. A significant percentage of these before giving birth. But not me, it began deep within my ready-to-explode womb, when my stupid, faulty body refused to give life in the way that it is supposed to.

Mine and Wolfgang's birth story began in the most difficult of circumstances. Awash with blood, pain, exhaustion and completely at the mercy of strangers. I was beginning to turn yellow; I was so ill my organs were beginning to fail. I was the kind of yellow I would expect to get from relying on uber-cheap cider for my daily nutrition.

If my love of wine becomes something more ominous, at least I know what I look like with an alky's[14] tan and a beer belly, I thought to myself.

The bottle green medical sheet which separated Top Me from Bottom Me saved me from having to actually see what was going on. But I felt it. I felt every tear, every cut. I say felt because I did feel it. It didn't hurt but I was completely aware of it. It felt like they had cut a hole in my torso which was about the same size as a beach ball, from just under my boobs to my pubic bone. I would swear that's how big the opening was (I later discovered it wasn't, but that's what it felt like). Once they had cut me open, I began to feel what I can only describe as seventeen arms, up to their elbows, rummaging and ripping in my stomach cavity, as if they were trying to find the telly stick down the back of the sofa. The seventeen arms froze each time I heaved, throwing up sideways into some sort of cardboard receptacle.

All of a sudden, dragged from my stupid body, there he was. He was born. I expected to hear trumpets, birdsong or violins, see shooting stars and love hearts floating about, but I was too busy throwing up sideways, and going out of my mind.

Baby Wolfgang was born. And my world turned upside down instantly. If you can call a three-day fucking labour instant that is?

I watched as Wolfie surfaced, upside down from behind the curtain and was held up by two arms. All I clearly remember was that he emerged a dark and angry purple.

---

[14] I am aware that this is an immoral, judgemental, awful thing to say. In my defence, I wasn't myself at that time.

Purple baby and yellow mother. Tinky Winky meet your mother, La La. My son was born at 8.09pm, weighing 6lb 15 and a frickin' half oz. Why couldn't the inconsiderate little git be 7lb? It took me years to remember the date and time and weight! Drugs and trauma do not clear memories make.

Due to my predicament of being tilted upside down a bit, throwing up sideways and not being properly joined to the lower half of my body, the nurses gave our boy to his daddy for the first skin to skin contact. I tried to see him, to touch him, but I couldn't move. After a few minutes Fernando began to go a funny green colour (Tinky Winky meet your father Dipsy - just missing Po now!) I watched in sideways disbelief as he handed our boy over to a nurse, because he wasn't feeling well. Poor old Fernando. Fernando is a big chap, as I've already mentioned, and I think that the young male nurse was a bit frightened of Fernando flattening him if he fainted, so he plonked him in a wheelchair.

Really Fernando???
Fucking Really?????????

My face folded into a scowl and in between my heaves, I furiously loathed poor old Fernando as he was being tended to. I watched him being wheel-chaired out of theatre by a nurse, from my sideways and upside-down position.

If looks could kill, I reckon he, the nurse and half the hospital would have been obliterated by my face. Apparently, he was okay a few minutes later because he had laid down on the floor outside the theatre to *cool his face*. The idiot wasn't allowed back into theatre after contaminating himself on the floor, pressing his cheek to the cold tiles.

Eventually, I was handed my baby. I hear of the moment that mothers meet their new babies for the first time. Fireworks explode and they securely bond as they gaze into each other's eyes. I did not experience the emotional imprinting I had read about, the beginning of the healthy attachment I was supposed to know about.

I was promised this special moment by nature and by the generations of mothers before me.

I held my baby close in anticipation, and I felt... nothing. Very little at all, apart from a weak little flutter of the need to protect this little purple thing. Between the trauma and probably the copious amounts of drugs I was pumped full of, I seemed incapable of feeling my emotions. But I could still think. Actually, my first thought was that he had this strange, purple woolly hat on.

That's not his hat. That's not our hat, it's the wrong fucking hat! That's not the hat I specially chose for him to wear when he's first born. Will nothing go right?

It was pedantic I know, but control over every tiny aspect of his birth had been taken away from me. The procedures felt like they had been done to me, not for me. I felt as if I had been violated, as if I'd been subjected to it all. I was completely void of emotion. Probably because if I hadn't been completely shut down, I would have screamed and screamed and screamed; the nurse hovering next to me would have probably suggested they wheel me to the Psych ward rather than back up to Maternity.

I clung to Wolfgang and thankfully a tiny but real emotional response did seep through into me, although I barely felt it at the time. When I properly looked at him for the first time, I noticed my son had beautiful dark blue eyes. I remember thinking I have never seen anyone with such amazing coloured eyes before. Dark as a stormy sea and spotted with gold. Such a small pause in a dangerous, ferocious storm, and I cherish this memory.

The next second I was back in a surreal state of panic, as the bed mysteriously began to move and I realised we were being pushed out of the theatre. A gush of cold air hit me in the face as we went through some double doors where we found Dick Van Cheek-Cooler anxiously waiting. With my baby in my arms, it was the strangest journey of my life. Everything seemed so surreal. I remember the temperature changing as we went through lots of doors, warm and then cold and then warm again.

We arrived back on the maternity ward and were taken to a side room. I imagine these moments were special, but I cannot remember them, not at all. Which still makes me want to cry.

All I really remember is Sunshine taking photographs of me as I drifted drowsily between asleep and awake, clutching the baby, terrified I would drop him. His hat had miraculously changed by then too. Fernando and Sunshine must have gone home at some point because I remember noticing all of a sudden that they weren't there.

My next memory is much later when it was all dark and quiet (as quiet as a hospital ever is) and my baby was fast asleep. Every time I drifted off to sleep some nurse would come and take my temperature or my blood pressure. As soon as I closed my eyes a beep of some twatting machine would wake me. The last straw arrived in the bulbous shape of she who I will call Cruella Shipman (wife of Harold), a scary night shift midwife with an enormous bosom, shot-putter's calves and an attitude to match. I reckon they only put her on night shifts so you couldn't see her properly in the dimmed lights when she whispered scary shit in your ear.

'Come on girl, let's give that nipple a bit of a pinch and get it flowing.'

Breastfeeding is… oh just Fuck Off. Before anybody starts shouting at me, I think that breastfeeding is beautiful. I get it, I really do. All through my pregnancy I had wanted to try. As well as nutritionally, I knew how important it was for bonding and attachment.

But I wasn't breastfed, and I'm completely cool about it. Admittedly, I am a half-wit on occasions, but I don't think that's caused by what type of milk I was fed. I'm not a serial killer, or ever done anything particularly evil (although I guess calling Fernando a lethargic pig isn't very nice). And up until the very last antenatal class, I had always felt quite relaxed about breastfeeding. I wanted to breastfeed but if it didn't happen, as long as baby was fed, I would be okay about it. The pressure surreptitiously began a bit at that antenatal class, and as for feeling relaxed about it, well it was a shockingly different case after he was born.

Three breastfeeding mothers came along to that last antenatal class to talk to us about it. I will call them Boob, Tit and Swinger. Boob, Tit and Swinger talked about a breastfeeding support group they were setting up. Why breastfeeding mothers should need a support group was a mystery to me at that point.

Isn't it just a case of point and squirt? I had wondered.

I beamed at these three ladies, proud to be a woman and proud of the fantasy breastfeeding mother I would surely become, I wanted to be part of their clan. I wanted to be a good mother, just like Boob, Tit and Swinger. They made it sound simple, just as nature intended, never once did they talk about the possibility that sometimes, milk just doesn't come. Not a single time did I realise that my milk might not come. Bottle feeding wasn't even mentioned. They instilled in me another expectation, a demand of my body. I was absolutely determined I was going to breastfeed. No doubt about it. If Boob, Tit and Swinger could do it, so could I.

However, in that dark, surreal room, having just given birth, it was my turn to try and breastfeed, and it simply wasn't as easy as that.

Cruella's bosom squashed me to within an inch of my life as she hunched over me. As much as I really wanted to breastfeed, Cruella was fucking demented with determination that I was going to. Before she arrived in that dark little room, things had started getting a tiny bit better. But as soon as I'd settled into that tiny bit of calm, Cruella ensured that my crazyometer was back to pointing back at Terrified.

Imagine being sliced in half by a shockingly incompetent magician, then three hours later, a gigantic-bosomed nurse called Cruella Shipman grabs, pokes, pinches and squeezes your nipples with frightening determination. This is illegal everywhere but on a maternity ward. You can't fight back, because you are told very firmly that all that's what's supposed to happen, I couldn't really move to escape her prodding and pinching anyway, because her boobs ensured I was pinned to the fucking bed.

It was so, so awful, I felt violently assaulted. My milk wouldn't come. Cruella treated me like I was refusing to do it. It was brutal. As she poked and grabbed, I wondered if the horrid old bitch was on the Sex Offenders Register. She definitely should have been. Nothing came out apart from a few drops. Cruella flatly refused to give me a bottle for him. She really couldn't have made me any more frightened or disturbed if she tried. I hadn't slept for three days and I was clearly in shock due to the emergency C-section. Looking back, I think I learnt what it must feel like for a dairy cow. In fear for her life, about to be made into burgers because she can't make any milk. I am still unable to look at a pint of milk without remembering where it came from and feeling sorry for the poor cow.

Eventually the awful bitch gave in and brought me a tiny little cup of formula milk. I managed to cup feed Wolfgang a little and he went back to sleep. I sat on the hospital bed in my ridiculous dressing gown in the dark room full of blinking lights and beeps. I just stared at my son sleeping in the cot. My mind was blank. No love, no happiness.

The training I'd had in trauma and Post Traumatic Stress Disorder equipped me to deal with this sort of thing in other people, in someone else I would have recognised it straight away. Alas, I didn't realise it was happening to me. I thought everyone's birth was like this, and that I was just weak and defective. I can see now that I was utterly traumatised, my body still completely within the fight, flight or freeze response. I was completely frozen, a petrified smile on my face, but my brain, my abdomen and my heart were all broken.

The next day Wolfgang and I were put on the ward with other new mothers. I was knackered, my body was in shock and my milk wouldn't come at all. Hard as I tried, I was unable to feed him myself, nothing was coming out.

Although I'm not much enamoured with the rest of my body, I have a good set of boobs, look fab in a push up bra, but apparently completely useless at doing what they were created for.

Sunshine was fuming at the state of affairs and told me not to worry and to bottle feed him[15]. I finally managed to gain a little bit of control by realising she was right. I took her advice and explained that I wanted to bottle feed him. The judgemental looks on the nurses' faces were awful when I

_____

[15] Thank you, Sunshine, you will never know how grateful I was for your support at that moment.

110

informed them of my decision. It was as if I had decided to give him vodka. They refused to warm the milk for me and did everything they could to discourage me. Nurses and other mothers who berate people for not breastfeeding categorically disgust me, not only is it a mother's bloody choice but that judgement is especially harmful to the mental wellbeing of those whose milk just doesn't come. I fucking know.

What Boob, Tit and Swinger had started, Cruella and the other nurses finished. They made me feel that bottle-feeding was sinful, abhorrent. I had **failed** to proceed in labour, I had **failed** to give birth to my son naturally, and now I had **failed** to breastfeed. I truly believe that these failures were the seeds that began the growth and spiral of my mental health injury… and I see it as an injury; the traumatic birth the catalyst, and the whole process in the hospital was nourished by the judgement and shame the nurses heaped onto me for my so-called failures.

I bumped into Boob, Tit and Swinger in town quite often after Woolfgang was born. I would feel a hot, dark flush of shame run up and down my body, and scuttle away from them, feeling like a cockroach. I can say hello to them these days, without feeling shame, just about. I still don't remember their real names and it's got way past the point that I can now ask. They are just Boob, Tit and Swinger to me. I know they were doing their best to try and help. But if you are one of those nurses who made things difficult and shamed me in those early hours, take a bow. Especially you Cruella, you nipple-squeezing monster.

23

The Day After the Best Day of my Fucking Life

The following morning, we were moved out of the high dependency bit of Maternity and out of the relative safety of our private room. Cruella had finished her night shift. We were put in a ward full of normal mothers. My memories of that first day or so are extremely hazy but I do remember looking at the private room across the hall where I'd spent that horrific day after I'd lost the first baby. Different pregnancy, different circumstances, thankfully very different outcome, same terror.

Nobody checks new mothers for Post-Traumatic Stress Disorder. Why the fuck is that? Between 25 and 34 per cent of women report that their births were traumatic. That's about one in three of us. Most women who suffer with PTSD after a traumatic birth are diagnosed instead with postnatal depression and are prescribed medicine for postnatal depression, not treatment for PTSD. They are two distinctly different conditions and should be treated as such. The recommended way to treat PTSD is trauma-focussed physiological therapy. Looking back, I think I had both conditions and like I mentioned before, the reason I can't remember lots of details about Wolfgang's birth is that my poor brain was doing its best trying to protect me from the trauma.

When someone is involved in a traumatic situation, the amygdala - the clever bit of the brain that sorts out memories – can choose not to transfer short-term memory into the long-term memory storage bit. What it's trying to do it to protect you from the physiological and psychological effects of the memory. So it comes from a good place, but this for new mothers, is another difficulty to face; a mother who can't remember the first days of her son being born, on the most important day of her life?

I lay there in my ridiculously fancy dressing gown, clutching at this little bundle on my chest. I have a beautiful photograph of this moment, which I treasure, because behind those terrified eyes, I now see that I did love him, wanted to protect him and care for him. I just couldn't feel any of that at the time. Because behind the smile, I was utterly and completely lost. I was terrified of what had happened, of myself and how I was feeling, of my baby and how to look after him, of my C-section wound, of the nurses, of the noises, of my defective boobs, of, of, of… so I had shut down.

In my opinion, the element of lost control in a stressful situation is a big indicator of whether someone will develop PTSD. Some people survive trauma, abusive childhoods, natural disaster, bereavement and other horrific things, without being severely affected. They walk out of car crashes, out of war zones, out of hell. Some people really do. And they are pretty much okay. So why are some people okay but others are not?

I've got a theory.

In every case of trauma I've worked with, my client has either had no control to start with or has lost control in some way during the traumatic event. Exactly as I was. I believe having some control over a stressful situation is key to not being traumatised by it. Like the person who was able to walk out of a crashed car versus the person stuck in the car until they can be cut out by the fire brigade, the woman battered by her husband who was able to leave, rather than the one who has no choice but to stay… that sort of thing.

Control of every aspect of childbirth was taken away from me. Every decision I had made was changed by the professionals who were looking after me. I totally understand this had to be done to save our lives, I really do. But it was my body, and my child. Some of those decisions needed to be mine, in order for me to feel that I had some element of control.

But that didn't happen. For example, when my milk wouldn't come it was maybe because my body wasn't working properly. I tried to make a responsible decision to bottle feed, in order to make sure my son was nourished. I was made to feel humiliated and ashamed; my decision was challenged by the nurses at every feeding time.

A clear memory I do have of those days in hospital is when Hosenose came to visit us on the second day. She could see straight away that I wasn't completely there. She decided to take action to try to bring me back to myself and whispered in my ear.

'Look on the bright side… no baggy wizard's sleeve for you… woo hoo!'

I then noticed that somehow, as he lay in my sister's arms, Wolfgang had positioned his fingers so he was giving Hosenose the middle finger. It was epic. It was like a tiny glimmer of normality in me woke up. That was the very first time I felt like me, post-birth. I burst out laughing like a crazy thing, tears pouring from my eyes at both the relief that I still knew how to laugh, plus the excruciating pain in my abdomen that the laughing was causing! I think it was the moment that I first felt he was truly mine too. He was sticking his middle finger up at my sister, best friend, and lifelong victim of my evil sense of humour. It was the very first time I thought *maybe he really is mine?*

24
I need to go home...

Cruella mustn't have had any puppies to kill that night, because she was back working on the ward again. I dared to ask her when did she think Wolfgang and I might be able to go home? She pointedly told me that as soon as I could get out of bed and walk to the toilet I could go, the look on her face clearly indicated that I wouldn't be able to do it as I was clearly such a pathetic mess.

So I fucking did it. *Okay you witch*, I thought, *my tits and fanny aren't working properly but my legs fucking will!* I desperately needed to go home, to be in familiar surroundings. I needed to take my baby home, I needed my things, my dog and Fernando's cuddles on tap. So I did it. I got out of bed, resisted the urge to scream at the pain. I triple checked that the nurse knew I was leaving Wolfgang for a moment and staggered like Quasimodo to the toilet.

Standing up straight was totally out of the question, it was clearly impossible. I would never stand up straight again[16]. But the pain in my abdomen and the not being able to stand up straight was blotted out by this invisible bungee cord that appeared to be connecting me to the cot. I dithered, taking painful steps forwards then backwards again, and then forwards again, between the bed and the toilet.

I was terrified to leave my baby alone for even a second; terrified of what? I've no idea, but the thought terrified me. Perhaps I should have been elated that I was standing on my own two feet, but that terror blotted everything else out. I decided to go for it as quickly as I could and so I would run to

---

[16] Don't worry if this is how you are feeling, I promise I was standing up straight a couple of weeks later.

the toilet. So hunched over in two I hobbled to the toilet as fast as I could.

I got in there and wrestled with my clothes, wincing. When eventually I managed to lift my nightie up, I'm still amazed I managed to not completely freak out at the massive pressure bandage that was glued across my belly, curved like a sadistic smile. It was as hard as a piece of wood.

Then I had the delightful little job of trying to have a pee. Lowering myself onto the toilet., I got myself sat down and I managed to squirt a bit. I'd had the pleasure of being catheterised; so it stung like a bastard. I felt like I'd been repeatedly high-fived in the fairy by a fucking stinging nettle.

If anyone ever dares catheterise me again, I will do very bad things to them. This is not an idle threat.

Equally terrified and triumphant, I cautiously slid off the toilet and hobbled back to Wolfgang. I couldn't straighten up at all, I was convinced I would rip in half if I tried.

I did it all too early because I was determined to go home.

I spent the night in triumphant agony. Because this time I had beaten my useless body. *That'd show Cruella.* I could actually do something to make things better, it was agony, but if it meant I could go home then it was worth it. I can remember a bit from this time, because guess what… I had a little bit of control back.

The following morning, I had to ask for stronger pain relief. Cruella had gone home by this point, and the nurse who came to give me the medication gave me a massive bollocking for getting up too soon and insinuated that I had actually damaged my chances of going home early.

I really hate Cruella because of this. Thank god the following night the old cow wasn't on the night shift. Not because I would have said anything, I was so cowed at this point that I was broken, and nothing at all like my usual gobby self. One day, I'm going to find her. And I'm going to do bad things to her as well.

My herculean effort paid off, because twenty-four hours later, at last, Wolfgang was examined and discharged with a clean bill of health and they let us go home; forty-eight hours earlier than we should have done.

PART TWO

25
Home

I have never in my life breathed such a sigh of relief to be home. The sight of the place, the familiar smell of home, the familiar give in the sofa, it was so soothing. I remember that my house was covered in balloons and thinking that was a lovely gesture, I felt like a soldier welcomed home from the war. I have no real memories of that time, until about 5am the following morning. It was dark and eerily quiet. We were all downstairs and Wolfgang was asleep in his Moses basket. I was lying on one sofa looking at Fernando lying on the other one, flat out asleep, our dog laying on top of him, looking at me. The dog was probably wondering (as certainly I was) what the fuck had just happened? The confusion in her eyes was probably reflected in mine.

Against my will, I couldn't help but visualise creeping out of the house and speeding off in my car and running away. To where? I have no idea, just driving and driving and never stopping. Of course, I didn't but I felt like a monster for wanting to.

Talking about monsters, I had expected to come home with a bit of a Frankenfanny (a watermelon doesn't come out of a hosepipe without some serious damage), but no, my foof was in one piece (apart from the lovely post-catheter sting). I had another wounded area to think about. Underneath that scary pressure bandage, I was stapled together…

Bloody stapled!

Like with real metal fucking spiky staples. Metal staples. Like a fucking desk stapler that's used to attach paper together! What the fuck? Did the medical supplies run out, so the surgeon grabbed his fucking stapler off his desk? Am I so fucking worthless that they won't stich me up like a normal human being? A fucking stapler! Even a fucking Argos catalogue gets glued together. The staples kept me technically in one piece, but mentally I was in bits, my mind could have done with a few of those staples.

The midwife came a week later to remove them. How I didn't faint, vomit or just refuse I don't know. I can still hear them going 'plink' into that metal dish, one by one, as she took them out with her tweezers. Now I know it's common practice, but I didn't then. It was really shocking at the time.

Although I can remember bits, the first few days are a blur. I know I didn't take my bra off for a week after Wolfgang was born, I literally wore it for seven days, in the shower, in bed, everywhere. I was too scared to take it off. My boobs felt painfully hot and angry and weirdly felt like they were full of marbles (aha that's where my marbles must have gone!).

Still my milk didn't come… it never did. I remember my first shower, looking at my body. I didn't recognise myself at all. I felt like I'd been sawn in half. The pressure bandage was still on at this point. I was terrified to take that off as well. The water ran into my eyes as I sank to the floor, with a feral, silent scream as my unknowing family were crowded in the living room downstairs. I literally thought the end of my world had come. My mind didn't feel connection to my body, like I was just this jumble of scared consciousness. Like I was floating above everything that was happening.

I must have appeared ill, I must have. But nobody said anything to me about it, so I thought I was just being stupid or incompetent. I just got on with it. Gritting my teeth, getting on with the practical stuff and ignoring my feelings.

Sometime in that first week, I unpacked my hospital bag, I remembered that someone had given me a leaflet about becoming a new mother to come home with. It told me all sorts of useful and all sorts of useless stuff. It talked about my milk, about recovering from the birth. It told me I might experience some sadness and distress for a few days after baby was born. I knew that the baby blues are so common that it's considered a pretty normal thing to happen and should last no more than two weeks. I felt well prepared in case it happened. I kind of expected to be a bit teary and snotty, crying over silly things. I was even prepared for the dramatic waving of arms and the graceful, beautifully smudged mascara and teary eyes. Perhaps a little bit of gratifying martyrdom - I know, I know, I can be a right bell-end sometimes. I fully expected that if any of this happened, I would bounce back after the required amount of sympathy and wailing. If I only had the guts to remove this stinking bra I'd been wearing. If only I hadn't been cut in half. If only my milk had come. If only, if only, if only...

On the bottom of the leaflet there was a tiny section on mental health.

If you experience any of the following, please contact your GP:

Difficulty Sleeping
No shit. I have this tiny person who has decided I don't need to sleep anymore. Even when said tiny human is sleeping, I just stare at him, my brain swinging between wanting to run away, this extreme anxiety – just knowing that something bad was going to happen, wondering what the fuck had actually happened, and this painful, incomprehensible love.

Over or Under Eating

120

Chance would be a fine thing, one minute I'm starving because I've forgotten to eat for two days, the next minute I remember I'm still the size of a small hippo and probably should get my jaw wired closed.

Lack of interest in Sex

What the actual fuck? I'd just had a baby. I wasn't even sure if it was physically possible since giving birth. Would the slightest hint of passion cause my C-section scar to rip? Would my womb fall out and my intestines get wrapped around Fernando's neck or his nether regions? What if I killed him? What would the coroner record as his cause of his death?

Misadventure. Strangulation by small intestines?

Would I be done for manslaughter?? I was also totally freaked out as baby was lying approximately 40 cm from us. It was so weird, I felt like some sort of sex offender even thinking about it!

Instead, perhaps the leaflet should have this more useful disclaimer:

Don't waste your time reading me. Instead, put me next to the toilet for emergencies. In case you run out of toilet paper, which you will, because you will go backwards and forwards like a knob-head to the shop, doing mad things like losing your car and hiding behind stacks of bog roll, which you will repeatedly forget to actually buy.

The ridiculous checklist meant nothing to me. The leaflet had an unhelpful list of signs, but they weren't anything like the madness that consumed me. The madness of my body's hormonal change of pregnancy and giving birth was, I think, fertilised by the trauma of the actual birth. It all snaked into my head, slowly circling and crushing my potential happiness and connection with my baby. I felt like an alien. Surely not

121

everyone felt like this after having a baby? Where was the overwhelming love and contentment?

26
How-fucking-lucky-I-was

So as it does, this alien-in-her-stinking- bra's world kept turning and days turned into nights. Five days after Wolfie was born, it was Fernando's birthday, and although I was still in a hell of a mess, a tiny bit of my inner fire flickered back to life. I got out my make-up and dolled myself up to go out for a lunch. We got to the restaurant and I had the biggest glass of wine[17] I could get my hands on.

The mad thing is, a picture of me was taken at that meal, and I look completely normal in it, even, dare I say, a tiny bit yummy? I looked like me. And yet, just a mere 72 or so hours before I had looked like a zombie, dazed and confused as to why nobody else in the room has clocked on to the fact that she's a zombie.

I didn't feel sad. Snot and wailing didn't happen. The tears didn't come. Because nothing happened to me. Nothing at all. Within a crushing, screaming numbness, there was just a tiny seed of doubt that I was too tired and afraid to contemplate. A seed which was sadly, destined to grow into a massive tree of fear and bewilderment, shame and hopelessness.

It quietly crushed and destroyed my experiences in being a new mum. Over the next few weeks, I became unrecognisable to myself, my mind marked as much as the scars across my tummy. The panic, anxiety, tiredness, mania, and terrifying thoughts were completely and utterly overwhelming, ruining what people insufferably kept telling me were the happiest moments of my life. I brought this little human into the world, and the responsibility to care for him, as well as trying to

---

[17] According to The *Criminal Mastermind* I haven't really stopped drinking wine since that day. Don't listen to him though, I'm pretty sure I have a day off now and then.

remember how-lucky-I-was and how-wonderful-my-life-was-supposed-to-be was utterly nonsensical to me.

Everyone had a smile for me. Everyone had a tip. There were people in my house all the time. I felt invisible. Busy making coffee, busy changing nappies, busy bottle feeding. I felt I was completely invisible and yet at the same time completely under a microscope. I was crippled with anxiety at every little detail of looking after my baby. I was terrified of getting things wrong. At least if I was busy being terrified of getting things wrong and berating myself, I could ignore the deeper part of my mind.

27

WorkHead Vs HomeHead

The shit that I deal with, the horrors that I help children to process, the frustration of services not working properly, and all that jazz means that in order to sleep at night, in order to still see beauty and hope in the world, I have to have two heads (metaphorically, of course, I'm good but I don't think even I could sprout a new head on demand) which I call: WorkHead and HomeHead.

A week after she had come to remove my staples, the midwife was back to check on me again. She must have observed something wasn't quite right, or maybe they ask everyone, I don't know. She asked me to fill in a questionnaire about my mental health. Work head immediately sprang to life.

Oh….. mental health? Oh I understand this. She's trying to work out if I have lost my shit….

WorkHead answered some of the questions (come on now, you can't expect me to have been completely honest, mental health is my turf after all), it was quite funny actually, knowing exactly why she was asking these things. HomeHead must have been a bit more honest though because it turned out I scored a bit high for postnatal depression.

Yet nothing came of it. Nothing at all. Even though quite clearly something should have. You might think that WorkHead would be busy chilling by the pool while I was off on maternity leave, but over the next few months, it kept niggling at me, whispering… trying to tell me that something was wrong.

I should have been listening to WorkHead. Really, it was the only head I could trust; because by the looks of it HomeHead was seriously malfunctioning.

WorkHead quietly suspected postnatal depression whilst the quite clearly malfunctioning HomeHead quashed it as a possibility. I was deathly afraid of admitting it. If I admitted to myself that I had postnatal depression, I was failing. And I couldn't fail. I couldn't let Wolfie down.

PTSD symptoms and postnatal depression wasn't obvious to me, but it should have been to the people around me, shouldn't it? When Wolfie was around six months old, I found a video on my phone that had been taken by my niece Loobie, who was a toddler at the time. It's a video that goes on for about a minute and was shot a couple of days after we had come home from hospital. She had taken the opportunity to nick my phone and was messing around with the camera. The house was packed with visitors and Loobie slowly pans the camera round. She stops and zooms in on me. I am sitting in the corner, looking like I've just walked out of a car crash, eyes like saucers and I'm looking round the room as if I don't know anyone in it. I feel sorry for that me. The rest of the people in the video are all cooing over the baby and acting completely normal – how didn't they know?

28
Percentiles

A couple of days day after Fernando went back to work (Wolfgang was about three weeks old), I had to face getting us somewhere on our own. We were going to baby clinic to get Wolfgang weighed. On my own. Without Fernando. Argh.

It seemed like such a simple job, jump in the car, drive baby in his car seat to the clinic. Yes, I was driving from two weeks after my C-section. I am aware this was probably illegal and stupid.

I got my bag ready. I packed enough clothes for Wolfgang, nappies, emergency rations, milk, dummy, 8 packets of wet wipes, enough to keep us going for a month. I manoeuvred him and his massive car seat into the car, the enormous rucksack of his stuff on my back threatening to spill its contents everywhere), and clipped him into the car seat. I pushed his door shut and then realised I had left the sacred baby book in the house.

Argh! Shit! I looked at the house, then looked at the baby clipped in safely to the car seat in the house. I really didn't want to drag him back out of the car, seat and everything, to run to the house and grab the book and have to do it all again.

Like a spectator at a tennis match I looked back and forth, car, house, car, house. Was it legal to lock the baby in the car for me to run and get the book? Was it responsible? Would someone steal him? Should I manhandle the car seat back into the house with me? I made a snap decision because I was already running late. I locked the car and ran as fast as my legs would take me back into the house to get the book. I can't even describe how anxious I was. It's a good job I'm quite sure footed, I reckon if I had fallen down the stairs, running down them that fast, I would have broken my neck. It seemed that it was just my mind that was broken, my feet were surprisingly able to take the stairs two at a time, which is quite an achievement given the slightest slip and my C-section scar quite possibly would have ripped open again.

The clinic is only about a five-minute drive away and, still panting, I manhandled him out of the car and went in. Before I could sit in the waiting room and catch my breath, I was called in to the health visitor's room.

My mind whirled as my hands dealt with the drama of undressing him. As well as the madness of trying to get him there then trying to wrestle his clothes off him, this would be yet another opportunity for me to anxiously obsess about whether his dot was on the correct line and which weight percentile he was in. Percentiles… percentiles… per-fucking-cen-tiles. A pretty word, a word I enjoy saying, percentile, it has a nice ring to it, I think. Like the words oxymoron, crumpet, marshmallow or bumcrackers (I made that one up). The health visitor must have explained to me six times what percentiles mean. Bollocks. Now there's another of my favourite words. Which pretty much describes what I think of the percentiles system. Who in their right mind came up with that? How many sleep-deprived, punch-drunk mothers like me have nodded and pretended to understand when the health visitor cheerfully says

'All good, Baby is in the 57th percentile!'

Am I the only one who panicked when I was told shit like this?

'Well, his head is in the 99th percentile, and his length is in the 15th percentile. Ooh, hasn't he got big feet?!'

Oh, just fuck off!

I gave birth to fucking Tweetie Pie??

29
Dandelions

Wolfgang, Fernando and I live in a small town with one supermarket that, for the purposes of this book, we shall call Gossip & Groceries. Gossip & Groceries is how most local public information is passed around.

A few years before I became a mother, I disconcertingly discovered that I am known as *that Child Psycho Woman* by some of the shop assistants at Gossip & Groceries, which, if you didn't know what my job was would be an incredibly worrying nickname.

I was shopping in there once, when a shop assistant asked me if I would accompany her to the customer services desk. I nodded, mutely, wondering what the hell I had done. I hadn't stolen anything or run anyone over in the carpark. Whenever anyone asks me *'for a word'* I always react the same; I shit myself (metaphorically, not literally). I recognised the woman vaguely - when you've lived in a small town as long as I have, you either recognise or are related to pretty much everyone – but I didn't know her to speak to. We arrived at Gossip & Groceries' customer services desk, I was full of shame for a crime I wasn't aware of committing. I hadn't pooed on the floor[18], and I hadn't slipped anything inside my jacket, could my car have rolled into someone in the car park? Convinced I hadn't stolen anything, but equally convinced that I was in trouble, we arrived. There was another customer standing by the desk, again I recognised her, but I didn't really know her.

---

[18] This is not as unlikely as it seems. A local legend for all the wrong reasons, Lou Poo is a real person, (I've changed her name) famous in our town because back in the 80's she literally dropped her pants and pooed in the corner of a local shop. Totally true.

'Here she is, that woman I was telling you about. That child psycho….. child psycho woman… oh whatever it is, she fixes children,' said the customer services lady to the customer.

I shit you not, that's exactly what she said. I hadn't committed a crime; I had been asked to go to customer services to speak with the customer services assistant's friend (wow, that's a mouthful) …whose child had started wetting the bed. I breathed a sigh of relief and gave a little bit of advice. I can cope with a bit of bedwetting.

Honestly, it happens all the time. When Wolfgang was in in year three at school, I was picking him up from after-school club (skidding into the car park a few minutes before they close, as per usual) and the after-school club supervisor asked me that bloody question again.

'Can I have a word?'

Expecting her to tell me of some awful deed Wolfgang had committed, I nervously replied.

'Yes of course!'

'Okay so I want to ask you a question, and I think you will know the answer to it. I know what your job is,' she said, very seriously.

Oh god she thinks Wolfgang is insane, said my mind.

'Okaaaay?' said my voice.

'Is gambling a choice or an addiction?'

I wasn't expecting that.

WTF?? Has Wolfgang been on the school iPad, placing bets on Foxy Bingo??

'Uh, well…it depends on the context really, impact on the person, impact on the family, whether it's a hobby or a compulsive act, that sort of thing. I don't really work with gambling addiction, I'm afraid.' I reeled off.

'I had a row with my sister last night about her husband gambling… It says on your website that you work with

130

gambling,' she said, in an irrationally accusing tone, as if it was me who was the compulsive gambler.

'Oh really? I'll have to check that.'

I'm 100% sure it does not say that on my website. It says I work with substance misuse. In fact, at the time, unbeknown to me, for two whole months my so-called professional website had been sending visitors to a dodgy Chinese website that sells knickers. So where had she seen that I supposedly work with gamblers? I still don't know to this day.

People stop me when I'm not working all the bloody time to ask me about their little Johnny's bedwetting or little Susan's tantrums. I have actually gone to Gossip & Groceries in disguise a few times, hoodie pulled over my head and sunglasses firmly on my nose. It fools the parents, but I can't get away with it with the little ones. Occasionally I'm rugby tackled almost to the floor by tiny arms, shouting 'Its Baby Lunatic! My Play Ferapist!' which I don't really mind because it's actually quite cute.

In the early days ~~post-apocalypse~~ after Wolfie was born, I only went to bloody Gossip & Groceries when I absolutely had to. If it wasn't clients or worried parents- *ugh I'm on maternity leave...* it was Yummy Mummies. I would literally hide from The Yummies in there. I would spot them wafting their yumminess around and suddenly I would become very interested in the ingredients list of a bag of organic sprouts (in case you don't know, there are only two ingredients in organic sprouts; sprouts and horse shit). I remember checking out the instructions on a box of tampons in an attempt to pretend I hadn't seen a Yummy. Apparently nothing about the process of inserting tampons has changed since Mrs Ravioli, the school nurse, had given me the little bag of *goodies* in Year 7.

I would do anything to avoid catching the eye of anyone at Gossip & Groceries, most especially a Yummy. If I was staring at something absorbedly, I could pretend I hadn't seen them. Maybe they would leave me alone. It was very confusing, people I barely knew wanting to talk to me, sharing intimate stuff with me. They wanted to know stuff about me. Susan and her tantrums I could deal with, but often all I had in common with these people who wanted to talk to me was that we had had babies at the same time. I'm not sure they would have bothered with me otherwise. But these things appear to change when you have a baby. I was most definitely not a babe magnet. Woefully, Tom Hardy (Fernando is my current husband, Tom is my future one) never stopped for a chat about my tender malfunctioning breasts – but apparently Wolfie and I had become some sort of baby magnet. Everyone wanted to talk to me, but most of the time I really didn't want to talk to them. Because apart from not wanting to know about their internal stitches and bleeding nipples (I am retching and cringing even writing that – these awful things never happened to me thankfully), I thought I might get caught out.

They might find out I was a fraud. That I was an imposter.

Because, deep down in those scary dark places inside me, it felt as though Wolfie wasn't really mine. I felt like I had stolen him, and that any day, he would be taken away from me, because I wasn't a real mother. Because I didn't feel like a real mother. Irrationally, I felt like a criminal. Like I had snatched him, like I had sneaked out in the dead of night and stolen him from the house of someone more worthy, more deserving of him. I coldly knew, with crushing certainty; I was a pariah, an outcast, a deceiver. But I didn't know why I felt like that. He had definitely grown in my womb; I had a hideous scar to prove he'd come out of it.

I remember once, I hid in Gossip & Groceries for more than three hours. It was actually probably more like three minutes really, but it certainly felt longer. I was crouched behind a mountain of toilet rolls pretending to look at something, shopping trolley and Wolfie strategically tucked out of sight. I hid until I was sure that enough time passed in order for this particularly glorious Yummy Mummy to pay and fuck off. We shall call her Perfectia. She was the most beautiful, terrifying Yummy I ever had the misfortune to meet. I had a clear view of Perfectia through a crack in the toilet roll wall. I was in full-on stealth mode. I thought I saw her leave and wondered how I could get out from behind the toilet rolls without looking like a weirdo. I was confident that I had managed to avoid her impossibly beautiful face and slightly patronising voice.

I crept out from my safe place. I thought I had gotten away with it. But nope. A beautiful head, complete with perfectly messy bun, snaked round the corner of my protective wall of toilet roll; I was mistaken, Perfectia hadn't left at all. Fucktwattery.

'Hi! What are you doi..?'
I immediately slapped a stupid smile on my face and cut across her.

'Hi!' I replied in an equally singsong voice, probably coming across as slightly deranged. But I couldn't have her knowing what I'd been doing. What was I supposed to say?

Uh, I'm hiding from you behind these bog rolls, cos you make me feel like a troll and you scare the shit out of me with your perfect messy bun??

I was acutely aware of my greasy, scraped up hair and make-up free face, of the dark shadows under my eyes and the dog hair that covered my ripped leggings - too tired to remove dog hair and too skint to buy new ones with my ridiculously crap maternity leave budget.

After a quick chat, Perfectia sauntered off, head held high and a smile for all to see. Her pert arse in perfect pastel, cropped trousers sashayed gently down the aisle, leaving a trail of toe-curling yumminess. She walked away, hitting me in the face with invisible little puffs of shame, silently farting judgement at me with her every step. I took a deep breath, unwedged my wobbly arse from behind the toilet rolls, and slowly pushed my trolley to the till, feet dragging, eyes on the floor.

Dejected and traumatised yet again at how crap I was in comparison to this angel-like vision of what I thought I was supposed to be like. Concealing us hadn't worked, the toilet roll fortress didn't have a hope in hell. At the time it felt like an attack, but now I know, honestly, Perfectia was actually just being friendly. Heck, now I even wonder… was she feeling the same as me? If she was, she was doing a much better job of hiding it than I was.

These were the lengths I went to in order to try to stop feeling so bad, so alien, so ugly and disgusting when comparing myself to other mothers. In fact, disgusting is pretty much the theme of how I felt for most of the first twelve months of Wolfie's life. My clothes were never ironed, sometimes left unwashed and often simply wet-wiped clean.

Even basic personal hygiene escaped my attention as I was catapulted into the zombie-like state of sleep deprivation and relentlessness of new-baby-ism - is that a word? Is it? It bloody should be.

A lot of that first year is still a blur, but I do remember a particularly cringe-worthy occasion when I sank really low in the 'disgusting and most probably insane' department. A couple of weeks after the health visitor had told me that I'd given birth to Tweetie Pie, we were heading back there again to get him weighed at baby clinic. This time I was pushing Wolfie along in the pram. It was a lovely sunny day and despite it taking me three hours to leave the house[19], I was glad to be actually going somewhere. I was still walking slightly bent over as I pushed the pram; I still worried that I would tear in half if I stood up straight. So there I was, hobbling along with the pram, contemplating how he had fed this week and worrying about whether he had put on enough weight. This sort of thing consumed me. As I walked towards the clinic, my mind was frantically trying to calculate milk ounces and number of days, when suddenly my nose was alerted to a strange smell. I sniffed like a bloodhound as I tried to identify the source. Confused, I knew it wasn't a Wolfie poo.

I continued sniffing the air. I became outraged, thinking I must have driven my pram wheels through some irresponsible twat's dog shit again. I peered at the wheels, but they were clean. I can only describe the smell as regurgitated roadkill smothered in gone-off garlic sauce. It was the smell of insanity. Alarm bells began to ring in my head as the realisation slowly sank in. It was me, my putrid breath gently blowing back at my face with every step I took. Shit! I must have forgotten to brush my teeth. Fourteen coffees and no brushing of teeth. It was disgusting. I was disgusting.

To make matters worse, I possessed no chewing gum that I could possibly have used to disguise the smell. I⁹ had remembered to bring the sacred baby health book, twenty-eight nappies and fifteen emergency changes of clothing for Wolfie. I wondered frantically if wet wipes were edible, would chewing a wet wipe even disguise the smell and save me from shame? I hadn't picked up my purse. I couldn't even go and buy some mints. I frantically looked around for something to help me. My eyes rested on a splash of yellow. For a split second I really did consider having a chew on the only thing I could see that might be vaguely edible; some wilted dandelions scattered on

---

¹⁹ I'm not even exaggerating.

patch of scorched grass. I stood rooted to the spot. I stared at them, crazy thoughts running through my head.

Would it work? Would my breath smell better? Would I pee the bed? Are they even edible? Rabbits eat them, don't they?

It was a toss-up between arriving at baby clinic smelling like this or having a go at chewing the sad looking things, their muted yellow faces drooping towards the floor. I imagined my deranged smile and the worried health visitor, staring at the bits of yellow stuff sticking out of my teeth at all angles, her hand creeping towards the telephone to ring the appropriate person who would suggest they have me sectioned. I came to what little sense I still possessed and remembered that dogs tend to pee on dandelions. So I left them where they were. I continued on my way, acutely aware of the time and my smell.

Wow, I really did do postnatal insanity with aplomb.

I got to the clinic and the friendly receptionist, who for the sake of this book I will call Barbara, peered into the pram. Barbara was lovely but, in my current state of stinking breath and utter panic, she was standing way, fucking way, too close to me. Barbara cooed over Wolfie and I stretched my neck as far away from her as was possible. I'm pretty sure my spine was about to go into spasm. I nearly passed out, holding my breath in a vain attempt to hide the fact I smelt like I'd been licking a dog poo bin. I answered her questions with my mouth clamped shut, smiling, nodding and making some strange nasally noises. I was out of options, I was being practically touched up by a doctor's receptionist (sorry Barbara, I know you weren't really doing that at all, but that's how uncomfortable I felt). No way could I allow her to catch a whiff of my breath – what if she phoned social services? Would they feel that my baby was better off in foster care than living with this stinking imbecile who had only just managed to talk herself out of eating dandelions? It's exhausting even remembering and trying to make sense of that day. What the hell happened to me?

Eventually, Babs stepped away, and the world came back into focus as I was able to finally take a breath. I mentally slapped myself as the logical part of my mind bravely fought with the dandelion eating, insane one; the part of my mind rotten with post-natal depression. I knew deep down that Wolfie wouldn't be taken away because I had bad breath, but after this I tried a bit harder to look and smell a bit less like I spent the previous night sleeping in a hedge, my face pressed against the dog poo bin.

After a few months of maternity leave, it began to get a bit easier to remember to brush my teeth. I even managed a shower occasionally and began to feel kind of ready to face the world. Six months into my maternity leave I received a nice email from my boss inviting me to a training day, and I decided that heading back to work for a Keeping in Touch Day would be a positive thing. It wasn't a requirement, but I thought a bit of normality would do me good, and it would be lovely to see all my colleagues again. It would be nice to put make up and smart clothes on, and who knew? It might stop my very last marble from rolling away from me and plopping through the drain that separates the sane world from the insane one.

30

A Green-Eyebrowed Monster

Nothing...

...can prepare you for the sleep deprivation that accompanies having a baby. I thought I was pretty hard-core before having Wolfie. I could pull the odd all-nighter to complete an essay and even get hammered two nights on the trot without feeling too bad. But I was wrong; I have discovered that I am a massive wimp when I don't get enough sleep. Oh, how I craved a nap, forty winks, a snooze, any sort of sleep. A pair of glasses with eyes painted on them didn't seem so ridiculous anymore. Pure, uninterrupted sleep was an unattainable dream, a memory of something I seriously hadn't appreciated before. I'm also a light sleeper, so every little thing woke me up, even when Wolfgang was sleeping.

Annoyingly, Fernando never had this problem, so in order to get any sleep, occasionally I would pretend I was still fast asleep and kick Fernando out of his coma-like state to greet Wolfie's middle-of-the-night wailing.

Looking back, I honestly don't know how we coped. How does anyone cope? I read somewhere that it's possible to die after 11 days straight of sleep deprivation. I felt like I was on day 11,000. Every... single...day.

I was so tired on the morning of that first Keeping in Touch Day. Fernando was taking Wolfie to my mum's. I waved them off and then I sat on the floor in front of the mirror to do my make-up. I'd forgotten to turn the big light on before sitting down, and I was just too exhausted to get back up and flick the switch. So I just did it, in the dim wintery morning light. I thought it would be fine, but how wrong I was! I carefully applied my make-up, my almost permanent yawn very helpfully causing a perfect facial position for the correct application of my mascara. Proudly I got dressed and got ready to leave the house, feeling rather normal for a change…

Holy fucking shit….! I cannot explain how grateful I am that something in the corner of my eye caused me to flick a glance at my reflection in the hallway mirror, just before stepping out the front door. I stared at myself, trying to work out what was wrong. My eyebrows were drawn on and perfectly shaped. They were also a lovely shade of emerald. I had green eyebrows. I had mixed up eyeliner and eyebrow pencil. A wet wipe saved my life. I furiously scrubbed them until they were back to mousy coloured and sticking out in all directions, but at least they weren't green. I will never underestimate restorative power of wet wipes again. Most annoyingly, I have never managed to get my eyebrows that perfectly shaped again either.

I'm already cringing at what I'm about to tell you next…The eyebrows weren't the worst bit of that day. Not by a long shot...

The combination of sleep deprivation and postnatal depression did weird things to my sense of humour. Hosenose said that in the first couple of months I would laugh longer and harder than was normal (I have a bit of a strange laugh anyway), snorting like a hysterical pig, with a sort of delirious glaze in my eye. Sometimes I would burst out laughing, tears streaming down my face at something nobody else found that funny. Or even funny at all…

Sporting suspiciously spiky but normal-hued eyebrows, I got to work that day and sat down with my colleagues for the meeting… it all felt very surreal. We began watching a presentation by a distant colleague which was quite boring. About halfway through the presentation, all of a sudden, my mouth opened, and before I knew what I had done, I'd cracked a horrifically, horrifically, horrifically (I could write horrifically a thousand times and it still wouldn't convey the extent of my horror), inappropriate joke, during which I kind of compared the presenting colleague to the recently outed paedophile Jimmy Savile. I sat there snorting and giggling like a crazy person. Needless to say, I was the only one laughing. I still cringe horribly about this and I'm astounded that I didn't get the sack. The topic was never discussed again. I sure as hell wasn't going to bring it up.

The only person who wasn't totally shocked that I'd done this was Hosenose, for Hosenose generally thinks I'm off my trolley anyway. About a year after Wolfie was born, with her somewhat scornful wisdom, she brought something else important to my attention. A really obvious fact really, in hindsight, that eluded me until I began to realise I had postnatal depression.

Hormones change me, they really affect me mentally. My conversations with Hosenose about this go along these lines.

'You do know you go completely fucking mental with your hormones, don't you?'

Well, that was a bolt out of the blue.

'Uh, no… not… always?' I will reply, somewhat offended.

'Yes, you do! One word, one fucking word… Gazebo!'

I am quite a careful person with money usually, but for a few days every month I will admit that I buy all sorts of mad shit. The first time I can ever remember doing this was when I walked into a garden centre for a look. Within 15 minutes I walked out, the proud new owner of a £900 wooden gazebo. I neither needed it nor had any use for it. I barely had a garden. I didn't even like it that much. I also didn't have £900 to spare. I had signed up to pay for it on a high interest monthly plan over like 24 years, so it was probably cost loads more… but no I'm not going there, besides, it will only give Hosenose more ammunition. I'm too scared to even consider how much it cost me in the end. I still have it; the fucking thing can last my whole life after that. Sometimes it looks at me, gloating. I never use it. It's there at the top of the garden, paint peeling, roof faded, as a mocking monument to my ridiculous hormonal spending habits.

My strange impulsive spending is sometimes so bad that I don't know I'm doing it until we are on a mad dash to somewhere two hours away because I've randomly bought something off eBay that I just needed. I usually drag Hosenose with me on these road trips, despite her loud and needlessly offensive protestations that there's something undoubtedly wrong with me, as she sarcastically berates me.

'Oh, is star week looming?' I drown her out with thoughts of how much my life is going to change for the better when I have my perfect new plastic chandeliers. It has taken a decade but I'm starting to see what she means[20].

---

[20] There's a catalogue of weird things I've spent my cash on. The most recent purchase is a combined result of my being on star week, and the conniving, bastard, misleading advertising of an online shop trying to take advantage of me and my insecurities. I naively bought what I thought was a sexy dress for our upcoming anniversary date night. I chose it because it was leather, yes, I know how it sounds, but in the picture it looked classy. It said it would suck me in and smooth my bumps. I wanted to dress up for Fernando for once. It arrived all the way from China yesterday. Bastard thing. I think even a self-respecting lady of the night would turn her nose up at it. It's gone straight into the fancy dress box just in case anyone ever throws a rocky horror show party. That's how awful it was. Bastards. I might as well have taken my £20, ripped it into tiny little pieces and eaten it... less calories than what I normally eat and maybe if I changed to a paper-based diet, I might've bloody fitted into one of my pre-*Wolfie* dresses, in the first bloody place.

31
Hurting

Hosenose, Sleepless Beauty and Fernando could see I was hurting. Under their watchful eyes, the world turned and I carried on fighting. My inner she-wolf was getting a tiny bit stronger by the day and I started feeling angry and resentful about why it had all happened in the first place. How it had all gone so wrong. Apart from having a bit of a disposition for being mad anyway I now am certain that the experience of giving birth was the actual trigger.

In this day of technological advancement, you would think that labour should be so much easier. Maybe a pregnancy chip in your arm, two pushes, a bleep and a perfectly timed pelvic floor squeeze. Maternity wards across the world should be full of babies flying out of stress-free vaginas, deftly caught by the grinning midwives who need more rugby-ball catching skills than medical knowledge.

For me it felt like a Victorian and barbaric process, and from what I can see it doesn't really appear to have changed much in 100 years. A traumatic birth can mean different things for different people. For example, being cut open, long drawn-out labours, assisted births, or your baby needing to spend time in the special care baby unit. A lot of mothers I know suffered some kind of trauma during birth, and quite a few of them developed post-natal depression.

The thought that my failure to emotionally attach to my son was excruciating. It was his opportunity to learn about other humans, his first proper relationship. I was terrified that I had fucked it all up. The guilt and shame ate at me and probably fuelled the anger and ultimately my poor mental health during

142

the first few years. Because if my own brain couldn't make sense of it all, how was his vulnerable little baby brain supposed to understand? I drove myself insane thinking if I fucked it up there was no going back, there was no repair and there would be no forgiveness. My little boy would grow up to hate me.

Babies are born with innocent eyes. Everything they learn is from their close humans. Our ability to make sense of other people begins to be created in that first very early bond between parent and baby. This is the foundation on which the child builds their experience, understanding and expectation of its interaction with other humans. New-born babies are biologically programmed to attach to their primary carers. They have no choice whatsoever. Forming this emotional bond is what ensures their survival, that they are kept warm, fed and their brains develop properly in the backwards and forwards dance of interaction between parent and child. This is why babies, puppies, and kittens are cute, with big eyes and pathetic little meows[21,] or, as in the case of humans, gorgeous little gurgles. It's why new-born babies' heads smell so nice.

When you really think about it, it's a bit manipulative if you ask me... bloody babies.

---

[21] 1f your baby (rather than your kitten) is meowing, seek medical advice urgently!

32
Forfucksake

Forfuck'sakenowmyspacebarbuttonisbroken.Afewchaptersinand
nowthis.ThisiswhatmylifeislikeALLthetime.Ican'tthinkofabetter
metaphoractually.Becomingamotherformewasjustliketryingtowri
teafuckingbookwithoutapissingspacebarbutton.

Phew. Thanks for fixing the space bar button Fernando, my
love god and handyman.

Oooh   spaces…   I
missed   you.

33
Guess who's back?

To be fair, I don't think my postnatal depression was helped by my old friend Endometriosis either. When Wolfgang was about six months old, the symptoms I had experienced prior to having him returned with a vengeance[22]. The teeth marks were back on the toilet door and I began to bleed for weeks at a time. My shoulder began its monthly screaming pain once again. Looking back, I realise now I really was a bit of a wreck.

Endometriosis is a hormonal disease and by now you know what hormone changes do to me.

'What are we?'

'HORMONES!!!'

'What do we do?'

'DRIVE BABY LUNATIC MAD!!!!!'

Thankfully, by now, the local ~~butcher~~ gynaecologist had realised that my endometriosis symptoms were not the run-of-the-mill whip-the-uterus-out, and that my disease was very advanced and complex. I was diagnosed with Stage 4 Endometriosis and with the help of FTWW Fair Treatment for the Women of Wales, I was referred to a specialist over in England[23].

---

[22] I can't say this enough. Having a baby does not cure endometriosis, despite the fact that lots of old fashioned tithead doctors will tell you it does. My symptoms were actually worse after having a baby.

[23] There is *one* endometriosis specialist for the whole of Wales. To put that in perspective, Endometriosis is as common in Welsh women as Diabetes, and our hospitals have whole departments dedicated to the disease. The one specialist that we do have is a four-hour drive away from where I live, and in a different health board so you can't get referred there anyway.

34

Splishy Splashy Slime

It was hard. I was bleeding a lot and managing this bloody disease - pun intended - as well as trying to manage the pressure I was putting on myself to be the perfect parent. There were times where I could barely stand up. I was in increasing pain from the quickly returning Endometriosis. The pain was back, like having a migraine in my shoulder and now it felt like I had a blowtorch pointed at my pelvis too. My mind was hurting so much as well. I tried so hard being a good mother to Wolfgang. I really did. But no matter how hard I tried, it just never seemed to happen. I just couldn't fucking do it. It seemed so important. At the time there were no funny groups on Facebook celebrating our individuality and supporting each other with humour and understanding. There was just this enormous pressure to be perfect. My trousers looked shit, my hair never behaved, and there was always mud (sometimes dog shit) on the wheels of my pram. I could have accepted this stuff though, if I could have believed I was a great mum in other ways. But I didn't believe it, not one bit.

When Wolfie was about eight months old, I decided we would try and make baby sensory slime... it seemed like a good idea, something simple that we could do together, fun, bonding, quality time and helping him with his sensory development. Surely I couldn't get it wrong? According to the internet, the instructions were simple enough. But slime making took up my entire day... foolishly I wasted a whole bloody day of my precious maternity leave. I drove ten miles out of my way to buy the ingredients. Three different bastard shops – baby seat in, baby seat out of the car each time. I checked the list again on my phone and realised that Google had given me an American list of ingredients, including one item called borax, which for some bizarre reason is perfectly legal in the US but completely illegal in the UK. That's why the bastard stuff wasn't stocked at shop number one or shop number two. I got out of the car at shop number three. I finally cracked. My left eye started twitching. Through my teeth I asked the bloke in the third shop for help. He cheerfully suggested an alternative. I triumphantly left the shop with my purchase and strapped Wolfie safely back in the car. We drove home, me taking deep breaths and my purse eight quid lighter.

Sensory play is really important for the development of babies, particularly before they can communicate verbally. Before language comes along, babies learn by touching, tasting, smelling, seeing and hearing the world around them. They experience the world and they learn about what is safe though their senses. They even begin to use their senses before they are born, listening to their mother's voice and heartbeat. It's my job to know how important sensory play is; I was desperately trying to do the right thing.

On that day Wolfie and I spent two hours in the kitchen trying to make the first batch of sensory slime. After the first hour of helping me, he retired to the highchair and watched as I struggled to stir it. I almost snapped the wooden spoon trying to mix the sticky concrete-like substance. It had the consistency of powdery goo with really hard lumps… I threw it in the bin.

Two hours again on the second pissing batch. The alternative ingredient hadn't done its job. I think if I had seen that cheery shop bloke, after wrapping the wooden spoon around his head, I would have made him eat our slime. By now, my poor left eye was strobing like a disco light.

At this point, my best plan might have been to repeatedly slam my head in the fridge door and make the slime out of my mushed-up brain, adding the required interesting texture with bits of my smashed skull. Taking a deep breath, I reminded myself of how important sensory play was, I persevered with gritted teeth. A fake smile on my face and the odd cheery comment to Wolfie about how much fun we were having. It wasn't fun and it didn't even work. The second slime attempt wasn't the least bit slimy, and ended up with the first batch, in the bin. The moment the so-called slime thudded to the bottom of the bin, I noticed that Wolfgang had somehow managed to get the lid off his sippy cup and had poured it all over his tray. He was licking it up like a dog. He lifted his head, turned to look at me, and started screeching 'Splish Splash!' over and over again, whilst slapping his hands in the drink. I could feel the mania building inside of me. Suddenly my hands started slapping the tray too, I was laughing and crying at the same time, copying him and shouting 'Splish Splash!' like a lunatic. He loved it. We were both covered in the baby drink. It was all over the floor and splattered up the patio window. I came to my senses (what senses I had left) and began clearing up. I plonked him in front of *In the Night Garden*, and hid out of his sight while the tears came.

I cried my eyes out. I just couldn't bloody do it. And for the whole of the first two years of motherhood, that's exactly how I felt about all of it… motherhood, this thing that I just couldn't do... I felt faulty, like I needed to be sent back to the shop and replaced on the guarantee. My batteries hadn't run out; they had never been put in the right way round to begin with! I knew how to do it, I knew why to do it, but I just couldn't bloody do it. I thought my brain just wasn't wired right. I'm a children's fucking therapist for fuck sake! A bloody play therapist! I work almost every bastard day with babies and children. Bonding with Wolfgang and making slime should have been second nature to me, but this time, for some reason, it wasn't working. I wasn't working.

Why was I finding it so difficult? Everyone else in the whole world seemed to be able to do it better than me. I should be doing it at least as well as them, if not a bit better. I was good at my job, so why was I so shit at being a mother? Why could I engage with other people's kids but not my own? And not just typical kids, but the most withdrawn, violent, traumatised ones? What the fuck was wrong with me?

What I now know is that Wolfgang didn't give a shit about the baby sensory slime, he didn't need it. What he needed, and ultimately got, was that moment of laughter and me mirroring him with my manic 'Splish! Splash!' action. Connecting like that was the important bit. But fuck me I didn't realise it at the time.

When I was pregnant, I optimistically thought I was going to be a Yummy Mummy. And then I wasn't. I wasn't even close. When I realised I wasn't able to be one, I used to watch the yummiest of mummies with envy - I secretly hated them for having their shit together. I saw them in their high, but sensibly so, wedges, with their trendy baby names and even trendier buggies, their perfect makeup and coordinating clothes.

Coordination… it was a miracle that my shoes coordinated with each other in those early days. Okay, let's be completely honest about this, sometimes I think it was touch and go that both my eyes coordinated and pointed in the same fucking direction. I was utterly demented with anxiety and sleep deprived.

Oh, and their bodies… they were so toned and tanned and skinny. How did they do that? How? Had they enrolled at the gym on the way home from the labour ward? Had a quick induction on the rowing machine with their new-borns clenched between their knees? On the lateral pull machine, with a twin baby securely latched and dangling from each nipple?

A friend of mine collects weird household items. One of these is a lampshade made out of a blowfish. A real, puffed up spiky, grey blowfish. It's so hideous, it's probably considered cool. I felt as exactly as attractive as that stuffed fucking blowfish, and nowhere near as cool. It felt as though those people whom I perceived to be yummy mummies were pushing their trendy buggies straight over my face. Tyre tracks all over my confidence in my maternal abilities; poking holes into my self-esteem with their smiles. They must have been shit at something; surely their lives can't be that effortless and successful …? I watched them like some sort of psychopath, wishing that they would spontaneously combust into a dusty, sticky mess of Johnsons' baby powder, glitter, breastmilk and the scorched remains of their sparkling white muslin squares. Oh, and just out of interest, why are we told to buy crap like muslin squares? What are they for? What can they do that wet wipes and kitchen roll can't? Another baby mystery that I never solved.

I'm deeply ashamed still to admit I hated everything about my life for the first few months of Wolfgang's existence. That's it. That's how bad it was. And I hated it, with a smile on my face. It would have been an atrocious and disgusting thing to say at the time but that's really how it was. Postnatal depression robbed me of any joy or happiness.

Babyloon Town is a lonely place. You are surrounded by other mothers and their bundles of joy. But you can't really see them, and they can't really see you. It's like one minute you are invisible, and yet the next (usually as soon as you have made the slightest mistake), you feel like you are made of bright, brash, neon colours that everyone can see.

When I lived there in Babyloon Town I felt like every other mother was normal, all apart from me. I was too terrified to say anything about the loneliness, even to myself. I know now that I wasn't alone, not in the slightest, but I had no idea at the time.

There seemed to be such a huge insurmountable difference between me and all other mothers. It seemed to have been distilled by my hurting mind into the simple fact that I was crap and everyone else was not. I felt like I was a germ under a microscope or a creature in a zoo, countless faces pressed against the glass, watching me. One false move would be witnessed by everyone. I thought I was so appalling a mother that something terrible was going to happen, every second of every day.

Terrified to make a mistake; I was broken and isolated. Because I thought it was just me, just who I was as a person. Not really cut out for it. I was gruesome, unnatural, not maternal, a freak of nature. Made even more painful by the knowledge that I was supposed to know what I was doing. They say: 'a little knowledge is a dangerous thing'… but for me, a bit more knowledge was absolutely treacherous. I knew that not bonding properly with my baby could do so much damage to him. I now know that we were bonding perfectly well, I wasn't gruesome or unnatural, or a freak of nature. I now know that you cannot be totally perfect or a total monster, nobody gets everything right.

Whether like me, it was death breath or rainbow eyebrows, every mother I have ever spoken to about this seems to have struggled with something. Even the yummy ones, when I stopped being so scared and hiding from them, I became brave enough to have a genuine conversation with them. Because becoming a mother is hard, even at the best of times. And it's okay now for me to say that.

At the time, I felt like I had to pretend it was the best time of my life. The constant feelings of sheer panic, the pretending, and the sleep deprivation made me do the craziest things. I used to repeatedly try to open the fridge by pointing and pressing the unlock button on my car key, getting pissed off when the fridge door didn't move of its own accord. Stupid fridge. Stupid car key. Stupid fucking me.

When Wolfgang was on his first settling in day at the childminders, I had a few hours to myself. I felt very odd, like I had left a vital part of myself, like my leg, somewhere. I felt so guilty for leaving him at the childminders. I felt like I'd failed him yet again, for even needing a childminder, even so I could go back to work to earn money to feed and clothe him. I tried during that few hours to relish a bit of time to myself. I decided to get a few jobs done.

I drove to the shop, bought a few things and enjoyed a leisurely walk home. I got home, stared at my drive for five whole minutes, vaguely thinking that something looked different. Then it clicked. Some fucker had stolen my car! I fumbled for my phone, ready to make the call to the police, I dialled, 9... 9... then I remembered…. Fuck! How had I lost something as big as a car?

Relentless mindless tasks, guessing what's wrong, second guessing yourself, listening to all the contradicting advice, burping, rocking, sleep training, changing nappies, constipation, shopping, mother and baby groups, dealing with sick, losing your car, healing from the birth, diarrhoea, trying to open the fridge with your car key instead of your hand, feeding, teething, constantly losing things, washing, cooking, cleaning, weaning, entertaining, teaching, new stuff, more stuff, nursery, reception, ever-changing, more, more, more… all on fourteen minutes of sleep per night!

But despite all the craziness, the sleep deprivation… it's all worth it, right? Because of the love you feel for that baby, the warm fuzzy feelings, the connection, and the bond… right?

For most mothers, it really is that simple. The relentless struggle is, quite simply… worth it. It's a small sacrifice for such a life-affirming reward. The feel of your child's arms wrapped around you blurs all the madness away, softens the edges of all the difficulty. But within the hordes of the typical sleep-deprived mothers who might very well still have crazy eyebrows or smelly breath, there is another kind.

The ones who might not have bonded with their babies as well, or perhaps don't have those fuzzy feelings. The ones struggling with not only the natural state of slight madness that comes with being a new parent but being stuck in the utter rabbit hole that comes with developing postnatal depression. The other ones who really, really struggle… like me. I was one of those other ones. I was functioning, I was parenting, I was actually being a bloody good mother to Wolfgang. I was loving him just the same as every other mother. On the outside it was all hunky dory, but on the inside I was screaming, failing and numb.

The wheel was turning, but the hamster was dead.

I couldn't see past the struggle, the daily grind needed to do something as simple as set a foot out of the house without two hours' preparation. I couldn't feel any good emotions, only the scary and overwhelming ones. I was an *other* one… I had terrifying thoughts and horrifying anxiety. I was one of the ones with postnatal depression.

The mothers who might despise themselves for thinking they weren't able to connect with their babies. The ones who may wonder sometimes if they even loved their babies at all. The ones like me, who believed my baby would be better off with someone else.

I actually thought that if I died, that my husband would have the opportunity to meet someone who would be a better mother to my son. Gut wrenching guilt that this beautiful, trusting little baby who had come to me, deserved far, far better than me. Irrational thoughts about how I could possibly give him what he needed – in my troubled mind, this didn't include me. I regularly had thoughts that adoption or even my accidental death. -anything would have been better than him growing up anywhere near me.

35

A Slug in the Wilderness

Postnatal depression? I wouldn't have it. Nah, like I said, that couldn't possibly be me, I wasn't ill! I couldn't afford myself the excuse of being ill! I was just a shit mother. I couldn't dignify this mess with a diagnosis. Because that would make it not my fault. Of course it was my own fault.

'I'm a shit mother.'

This was my mantra, my self-punishing aide-memoire, every hour of every single day for about two years. On the assumption that I was awake about 16 hours a day, my calculator informs me that I told myself this 11,392 times, completely drowning out and invalidating the many (but certainly not eleven thousand) times that Fernando and my family would tell me I was doing a good job.

My inner voice bullied and abused me for months. Silent to everyone else but screaming to me. This voice convinced me that everyone would be better off if I was dead.

That's right, I wanted to die, many times, not because I was suicidal, but so that Wolfgang wouldn't grow up with a monster for a mother. It was utter insanity, explosions of madness in my head. I wanted to die to save Wolfgang. How could I ever have thought that? The word depression doesn't even come close to that. Not even close.

I used to drive this mountainside road back and forth to work every day – Wolfie was about twelve months old by now and I'd returned to work after maternity leave. To one side of this road is an enormous drop. I remember feeling horrendous on a few occasions I was driving this road on my own. It's really scary thinking about those days.

On the first occasion, I was crying so much I couldn't properly see through my tears. I was probably running late home from work, worrying that I'd let him down yet again by being late to pick him up. I pulled over into a layby and banged my head repeatedly on the steering wheel. Still crying, I got out of the car and walked to the other side of the road. I looked down the drop. Could I make it look like an accident? Could I kill myself in a way that wouldn't look as if I had chosen to do it? An accident would allow Fernando and Wolfgang to get on with their lives without me. An accident would make them think I hadn't chosen to leave them. If I had an 'accident', I couldn't damage them anymore. I gave myself a mental slap and got back into the car.

It happened again on another two days. I wiggled the steering wheel towards the drop. Twice I wondered... But twice I steadied the steering wheel.

I couldn't do it. A person very dear to me lost their own mother to suicide. I have seen the effect, which I cannot put into words, both out of respect for my beautiful friend's privacy and because there are no words to describe what they experienced and continue to live through. So suicide was never, ever, a real intention. But my blood runs cold and the hair stands up on the back of my neck now as I write this. How it feels now, to even write that, is indescribable, as is so much of postnatal depression.

I also wondered how I would be punished for thinking like this. Would someone take him away? I've repeatedly seen the circumstances where children are removed from their birth families by social services. Horrific, sad stories. This wasn't the same. I knew on a cognitive level that he would never be taken away, but on an irrational, visceral level I expected a social worker's knock on the door each day. It is a very strange occurrence when your rational mind, your emotions and your instincts are at complete odds with each other. Why is the world so silent about this illness? Because it fucking exists. We know fuck all about it really, it seems to me to be different for everyone. It seems that postnatal depression is a bit distasteful to talk about or to admit to. Suffering seems to be unavoidable for new mothers.

Put up and shut up and make sure you are bloody grateful for such a beautiful baby. Get on with it.

I never read a leaflet that told me I might want to die in order to give my son a better life. What does postnatal depression even fucking mean? Nobody ever told me that this could happen. Not one person in all the nurses, doctors, midwives.   Boob, Tit, Swinger and the rest of society had implied that the next part of my life would be sublime, that having a baby would complete me. It was like they were the secret keepers of a wonderful club I was going to be part of.

I think society forgets that when a child is born, so is a mother. I know it's definitely not the same for everyone. I was supposed to be a caterpillar transforming into a butterfly. I was so confident whilst I was pregnant; I was definitely going to bloom from a non-mother-caterpillar into a totally natural and awesome mama-butterfly. But I failed to bloom, I just couldn't. I felt different to all other mothers. I wasn't a caterpillar on a journey. I was a slug, squashed by the cruel foot of life, my skin ripped open, my innards hanging out (that's what the C-section felt like), eaten by a twatting seagull and shat out into the wilderness.

I wonder now if my reluctance to consider that I had postnatal depression was down to a fear of losing control. The lesser of two evils. Perhaps being a shit mother was easier to consider than the fact that I was being played like a puppet by this cruel illness. Like if it was at least my fault for being shit, there was a reason for all this. I could work harder, clean the house more, attend more baby groups, dress more nicely, lose weight, cuddle him more, sing more songs, make more

157

homemade baby food, walk him in the pram more, drink ~~less~~ ~~wine~~ more water. More, better, cleaner, thinner, stronger, better, prettier, cleaner. More, more, more… perhaps I could do better!

Doing more, being a better mother felt easier to achieve than fighting my body's ridiculous responses to hormones. I had absolutely no idea how to fix it. So I drove myself even more insane trying to do all this, trying and failing to make myself into what I thought was the best, what I though was what I needed to be, a Yummy Mummy. But my problem wasn't that I wasn't a Yummy Mummy, my problem was that I was ill. Seriously ill.

Because I was supposed to be knowledgeable about mental health, I was supposed to know what I was doing. But I didn't. And I was terrified to admit it. Because surely then if I was faulty in my head, and I couldn't fix myself, I must be crap at my job also and that was the only thing left I felt confident in. So I kind of guess that I thought that admitting that I had postnatal depression would cause my whole world to come crumbling down.

It really needs to be highlighted that postnatal depression is a debilitating illness, just the same as mastitis, the flu, chicken pox, diabetes etc. We need to realise that as amazing as humans are, sometimes their bodies are crap, things just happen, it's not about blame, hormones go Ker-plunk and we lose our shit. And, a bit like autism, I believe it's definitely on a spectrum. I don't think you either have it or you don't. I also think you can slide in and out of that darkness.

In that darkness, the most terrifying thing for me was other people, particularly other parents. Nobody tells you how your social life can change once you have a child. You meet all kinds of people and suddenly have this thing in common with loads and loads of new people. I'm not callously referring to my baby here either, but this parenthood thing. And in this vulnerable state in the first year of having Wolfgang, I met loads of new people, got dragged along to stuff I didn't really want to be at. Funnily enough, now looking back I can see now that most of them were as utterly bonkers as I was.

I never went near Scarys. I was terrified of them.

I did, however make friends with some Yummies (Perfectia was the queen of this group) for a short period of time after the births of our babies. There was one girl in particular who I remember looking and repeatedly asking myself, what the fuck is she going on about?

I really had no idea what she was talking about. She continuously spoke-really-loudly-without-pausing-for-breath about shit I didn't understand or care about. I'm pretty sure she was a hand-dryer in a previous life. You know one of those blowy things in public toilets that are ridiculously loud and kids are scared of?

The-Human-Hand-Dryer and the other Yummies did nothing but slag each other off, gossip about people I didn't know, talk about celebrities and moan about their husbands, boyfriends or sperm donors (their charming words, not mine).

I realise now I had nothing in common with them. Nothing at all apart from a new baby. But yet again, I blamed myself, for not fitting in. Nights out with people I hardly knew, meetings at the pub, invites to the birthday party of children I had forgotten the name of etc. Barbeques in people's gardens, with a vague smile on my face, (usually wondering what the fuck I was doing here and pretending to like veggie sausages) feigning interest in the progress of the baby acid reflux saga of the equally neurotic mum (whose name I had forgotten) sitting next to me.

I could have had a whole conversation about baby related things in those days, without giving a fuck about who was sitting next to me or about their baby's acid reflux problem. I'd just smile and nod, and throw in the odd comment.

'Really?'

'Hmm, is it any cheaper in Aldi?'

'Have you spoken to the Health Visitor?'

These replies seemed to cover just about everything. After about twelve months and a very strange night out which I'll tell you about in a minute, I removed myself from this strange gaggle of mothers with whom I had nothing in common but the little beings we pushed around in our prams.

My brush with being in the Yummies' gang came to an abrupt end. It happened when I was invited on a night out with them.

The-Human-Hand-Dryer had been blasting incoherently at me for two hours. I nodded and sipped my vodka. I was getting quietly pissed. I continued to drink. I finally became pissed enough that I thought it would be a good idea to simply run away from her. Excusing myself to pop to the loo, I ended up at the bar, drinking shots with random people I didn't know, instead of returning to our deep and meaningful conversation, I had escaped.

Ohhhh vodka…. Ohhh freedom….

It felt so good. I found myself ecstatically head-banging on my own to the music the rock band were playing. The-Human-Hand-Dryer eventually found me, with a confused and disgusted look on her face, to tell me our taxi had arrived.

I didn't understand the Yummies at all. But that night, head banging and ignoring The-Human-Hand-Dryer, I had worked something out. I wasn't a Yummy, and when I realised that I wasn't, as usual my mind tried to blame myself. But something pushed back. No, hang on! I also realised that that woman really was full of shit, as coherent and intelligent as a fucking hand dryer, bless her. And that was about her, not me. I stared at her and a lightbulb came to life in my head.

'*Fuck. This. Shit.*'

Alcohol normally assists me to make very bad decisions, but for the first time ever, vodka had contributed to me making a good one.

I stopped seeing that group of people. I removed myself from their weird little WhatsApp group. I felt so much better after that. I see Perfectia and The-Human-Hand-Dryer occasionally (again, usually in fucking Gossip & Groceries), and I do a little smile which I hope says 'Hi! How are you? Lovely to see you, I hope you are well, now piss off, don't speak to me, have a nice day!' and carry on my merry way.

I realise that Perfectia probably wasn't perfect, and that she didn't direct her perfectness at me on purpose, just to throw my imperfectness into stark relief. They just were who they were, as I was who I was. They weren't my real friends. I had nothing in common with them. It was best I kept to my own kind of Mummy.

36
The Scrummies

I've got an awesome friend called Chainsawpixie. She is one of the most real people I've ever met. I now know that when her daughter Tweet was born fourteen years ago, she had felt like me after Wolfgang was born. But at the time I never knew.

I went to visit them not long after Tweet was born, and I remember being impressed at how laid back Chainsawpixie appeared with her baby. Tweet was lying propped in a bean bag (just a regular bean bag, not a fancy baby one) when I met her, and Chainsawpixie seemed relaxed. There wasn't tonnes of baby stuff in their house. It all seemed quite normal (probably why the memory stands out to me, because at the time I didn't think there was anything normal about having babies). This was around the time my friends and my sister had started jumping on the baby conveyor belt, back when even the word pregnant scared the shit out of me.

When Wolfie was about a year old, we went on a caravan holiday with Chainsawpixie, her husband, The Gruffalo, and their daughters Tweet and Fizz. Late one night, Chainsawpixie and I were having a couple of drinks in my caravan, just the two of us, watching over Wolfgang whilst he slept. We began talking about all stuff babies. Not that shite that the Yummies talked about, but the real shite.

Chainsawpixie told me how she had felt when Tweet had first come along, how she had suffered with low mood and anxiety…. I held my breath.

I nearly said the words.

'I think I have postnatal depression.'

I nearly told her. I hinted. But I just couldn't quite go there. Not yet. But what I gained from that conversation was that Chainsawpixie had opened the door. It wasn't just me.

As well as Chainsawpixie, I had my crew Sleepless Beauty, The Enforcer, Manykids and my sister Hosenose. Real friends were so important in my recovery from postnatal depression, and it was a blessing that I made a few more in the Scrummies.

From the day I met them (remember in Swimming for Hippos? Pubwatch soaring through the air…. Chickenkicker asking me about her piercing…?), they have been real. Like me, these beautiful idiots were stumbling through the journey into parenthood. Sleepless Beauty and I spent a lot of time with the Scrummies from when our babies were young, and as time went by, a few more beautiful idiots joined us. A wink or a quick hug from them helped me enormously to get through everything. They were prepared to reveal the crap bits as well as the good. They all struggled too with the emotional side of having a baby. They made me feel a bit more normal, from the very first day I met them. I can't ever thank them enough.

We are all still friends and I feel like I belong when I'm with them. We celebrate our friendship by getting really pissed together once or twice a year. We usually start off at a restaurant where we screech and howl our way through a meal and plenty of wine, becoming that table that annoys everyone in the place and nobody wants the table next to. As our babies have grown it's lovely to see us all maturing into Kid Lunatics.

In the early days, we would meet for coffee in each other's houses (never mine, because I was so hugely anxious about my house being a mess). I became comfortable and I bravely began to slip the odd comment about how I had been feeling into conversations with Sleepless Beauty and my new trusted friends.

Then suddenly, we all did. I began to feel that we were in it together. They really helped me recover, and I began to feel less ashamed. It was a lifeline. We began to exchange stories about our madness and struggles. We learned to laugh about it, we began to push back at the toxicity and silence. We took a big risk in confiding in each other. But we began to feel a tiny bit more comfortable in our new Mummy skins, because we knew each other's didn't fit right either. Being with Sleepless Beauty, Chickenkicker and Pubwatch, sharing our horrific and hilarious stories was like having an emotional colonic irrigation.

I remember the first day that I recognised my feelings of anxiety, shame and of just not being good enough in the eyes of another person. It was Pubwatch. Pubwatch was the first to let me in and the first Scrummie to join me in the private club in my head. Pubwatch and I bonded over my truck. This was the exact day that I began to understand that I was not alone. Late as usual, I turned up at a mummies' gathering when Wolfgang was about four months old. I pulled up in my fabulous truck[24], outside Sleepless Beauty's house. Pubwatch was washing up at the kitchen sink and spied my enormous vehicle through the window. When I eventually made it in from the car, she told me she wished she had my car so that she could ram the motherfuckers whose driving might put her baby's life at risk. I sort of laughed, and… I caught a glimpse of well, mad in her eye.

A look exchanged between us. And I knew. I just knew. She was like me. I wondered what else she was feeling, but at the time I was too scared to ask. I think she knew too, about me. But although I nearly did, I still couldn't say those words.

'I think I have postnatal depression.'

Pubwatch would have been the person I told, despite the fact I had only known her a few months. But I couldn't,

---

[24]Adrenaline junkie - or *mad bastard* if you ask Hosenose - that I am, I've always loved 4 x 4 vehicles and unlike yummy mummies, I actually drive them off road, through rivers, through bogs, and down dangerous tracks. It's a hobby of mine that I used to do a lot before Wolfgang was born and I bloody love it. Anyway, when I was about 30 weeks pregnant, I bought a ridiculously massive 4 x 4 truck (not for off-road driving before anyone judges me – even I'm not daft enough to go off-roading while pregnant or with a small infant).

because suddenly she disappeared off the radar. We all wondered where she was, nobody had heard from her for weeks. We began to worry.

37
Double-hard Bastard

Pubwatch had disappeared off the radar because she had been diagnosed with cancer. I cried my eyes out when I heard the news. She disappeared off the radar while she was processed the fact that she had been diagnosed with Non-Hodgkin's Lymphoma. I had just found her, connected, seen a bit of myself in her, we had become close and now I was going to lose her. I didn't even know her that well and I was devastated. How must her family be feeling? That was the day I realised that my dying was not the best thing for Wolfgang, when I began to imagine the impact of this on Pubwatch's beautiful family. I kicked myself up the arse and saw sense. My beautiful friend's awful diagnosis gave me some clarity.

Pubwatch's little boy was almost exactly the same age as Wolfgang. My heart broke for her and her beautiful son.

Why was life so terrible?

I really thought she was going to die.

Pubwatch couldn't leave the house for a long time. I used to visit her as much as I could. My heart used to hurt when I looked at my beautiful friend. She looked like shit, so ill, her body full of pipes, bloated and her hair gone from the chemotherapy. She always knew there was something wrong with me, but it remained unsaid, my lips tightly closed, I was unwilling to heap my problems onto hers.

When she recovered (because she is a double hard bastard), one day it all came out, and I told her just how bad I had been feeling with postnatal depression. She told me off for not telling her when I was feeling low. This is the woman who fought a life-threatening condition when our boys were tiny – telling me off for not telling her how I was feeling. *But I couldn't pal, I was scared you might die.* Your problems seemed slightly bigger than mine at the time, pal!

Thankfully even cancer is scared of Pubwatch. Took her on, tried his luck then fucked off with his tail between his legs.

38

Wheels

Anyway, thankfully this amazing woman is well again, and will kick my arse when she reads this. I can just imagine her telling me off.

'Don't be so soppy, I'm bloody fine now!'

The catalyst that caused Pubwatch and I to recognise a bit of mad in each other was my ridiculous truck. My truck was awesome to be fair, it wasn't far off being called a monster truck. It certainly wasn't a Chelsea Tractor; in fact, in my truck, I could have driven straight over the top of a Range Rover if I wanted to.

Why would I buy a massive 4 x4 truck I hear you ask? When it was heavy on fuel and ridiculous to park..? Well, of course it was so I could carry the tonnes of baby stuff that I was now responsible for. As well as all the other stuff, baby seats, prams, changing suitcase, I needed a massive truck so that I could carry around that bin bag full of essential fucking muslin squares.

No way was all that kit going to fit in a car. No way was I going to buy a bloody people carrier. I bought the biggest, meanest looking truck I could find. So I could carry my fucking muslin squares around and just in case I had to run over any Vauxhall Zafiras. I uh...kind of....accidentally... bought it when I'd originally gone out to look at a very sensible BMW. I'm not sure how that happened really. I think it was something to do with Slipalong. He's an impulsive petrol-head like me and I often get caught up in his enthusiasm.

Wolfgang was brought home from hospital in that truck. How the hell I got in the damn thing pregnant and then a few days later (recovering from a C-section!?) I'll never know. But I did. You will know by now I have some financial impulsivity issues when my hormones are not completely balanced. I know how this looks…! My truck was completely unsuitable and impractical but it was fucking awesome.

So my reasoning was that I wasn't prepared to buy a people carrier, and clearly, I needed an enormous car to carry all this ridiculous shit that comes with a baby[25].

My mad impulsiveness with cars struck again when I'd been driving round in my massive truck for eight months and the return-to-work date was looming. I couldn't use the truck for work as it was too expensive to run so we decided to buy a little car. But I took the little a bit too literally.

I'm not sure if it was my impulsive thing or my desperate need to stick two fingers up at conformity, but I went from one extreme to another. I bought a beautiful cream and black Volkswagen Beetle, a convertible… and only one type of buggy ever made fits in the boot.

Yet again I proved myself to be a bloody genius… the boot/buggy situation resulted in the kind-hearted Sleepless Beauty (who is probably still pissed off with me about this) driving The Bus an hour and a half out of her way to collect the only one I could find second hand. And it was total crap. It wobbled all over the place on its clearly insufficient three wheels.

Hosenose, in particular, hated this buggy so much that following an unreasonable outburst from her about how crap it

---

[25] I just have to say this. What the hell are we doing? Babies have fucking way too much stuff! *Wolfie* had five different beds before he was even born:

✓   Upstairs Moses Basket
✓   Downstairs Moses Basket
✓   Crib
✓   Cot
✓   Travel Cot

Is it just me or is this insane? I'm pretty sure that a few of generations ago my family members would have slept in a pulled-out drawer, with maybe a bit of blanket for padding? Or was that just my family?

was, I was forced to buy a four-wheeler buggy exclusively for use at her house. I think there was some deep-rooted buggy trauma at play here. Hosenose had a ~~hilarious~~ traumatic incident once when one of the wheels fell off her four wheeled buggy, leaving her stranded and having to balance the buggy laden with shopping on the three wheels. The funniest thing about this (she is my sibling so I am allowed to take the piss), is that like I mentioned earlier, she has dyspraxia and struggles to walk in a straight line at the best of times.

39

What the fuck is wrong with me?

Hosenose, Sleepless Beauty, The Enforcer and the rest of my people knew. Of course they knew. I finally began to know, and finally began to think about saying those six difficult words.

'I think I have postnatal depression.'

Sometimes, I could even think that maybe it wasn't my fault, if I had this thing, just sometimes.

Things slowly changed from blaming and shaming myself inside my own head to fixating on something else. If I did have this thing, how would Wolfgang be affected?

I began to agonise, convinced we weren't bonding. It was like Wolfie was on one side of a pane of glass, and I was on the other. Our palms were pressed together but the glass remained between them. Sometimes we could see each other. I could marvel at his beauty, see how cute he was, feel fluttering of deep emotional connection, but the next minute, it was like someone had pressed a button and the transparency of the glass would change. We were still either side of it, but we could no longer see each other through the cloudy, opaque wall. My mind would spiral into this excruciating anxiety because I couldn't see him anymore. I believe that postnatal depression was operating that switch, but still I blamed myself for what I thought was my unnatural response to motherhood.

I picked up my old research occasionally. I read through articles occasionally. But my symptoms didn't really fit. Could I possibly have postnatal depression? Could this madness, this insanity really be depression? It wasn't depression as I had learned to understand.

Postnatal depression is such a rubbish term for it. Depression seems such a gentle word for what I went through. And to be perfectly honest, the postnatal depression I experienced was a lot less about mood and more about intrusive and irrational thoughts, anxiety, numbness, terror, and disconnection not only to my baby but to everyone else. It was an incredibly lonely place. And it was this disconnection to my baby that terrified me most. I worried sick about his attachment. I hadn't the foggiest idea what to do about it, despite working with attachment problems so many times before. Because this time it was different. This time it was me.

I wonder now what other diagnoses I should have had. Postnatal depression, Post-Partum Dysphoria? Post-Traumatic Stress Disorder? I'm not convinced that these labels are actually helpful because everyone's experience appears to be so different. For example, laughing in a crazed way like I used to do – doesn't really fit with our traditional view of postnatal depression, does it? On one level I knew what was going on, on another I had no fucking idea. I liken it perhaps to a paramedic who knows he is having a heart attack. He knows the signs, he knows what must be done to save his life, but he cannot operate the defibrillator himself.

It's my job, how I earn my living… But could I save myself? Could I save us? Could I admit something was wrong? Could I even contemplate that me having postnatal depression might affect his attachment and what the consequences of that might be?

As a therapist, it's important for me to keep my own stuff out of my work so that the therapy I provide is really about my client's experience and not about issues I bring with me. Otherwise, therapists can become detached from their clients and stuck in their own experiences, which doesn't help the client at all. It's very difficult to be genuinely with a client if their stories just remind you of your own life and you get distracted in your own stuff.

Like a lot of therapists, in order for me to do a good job, I regularly have therapy myself. A lot of the people closest to me often don't know what's really going on with me because I am damn good at compartmentalising my life. I need to be able to do this because the horrific things I hear every working day would eventually cause me to become ill and unable to do my job – this is called secondary trauma and is a real risk in my profession. So I am used to dealing with my emotional shit in this very structured way. It's kind of part of the job. Because I do it this way, I don't often share the deep stuff with my nearest and dearest, I often don't ask for or seem to need any support myself, which I think is why most of the people around me had no idea that I was suffering like this. I suppose because of work, I was kind of in the habit of doing this, and I felt so ashamed I just couldn't. I couldn't even begin to explain at the time. I don't even think I could form the words to even begin to describe the shit show going on in my head. Until I slowly began to, thanks to the Scrummies.

Thankfully I slowly learned to stop treating my emotional self like a professional would, and I did eventually reveal my vulnerability to a few people, mainly my friends, the Scrummies. If anything has come out of all of this, it's that I now feel far more comfortable with my vulnerability[26] and far more able to show it.

For once, HomeHead listened to WorkHead. It was time to book myself in for some much needed therapy and sort my shit out.

---

[26] I'm not ashamed of what happened anymore - apart from the Jimmy Savile joke – I don't think there's any coming back from that one. Ever.

173

40
Therapist in Therapy

When Wolfgang was fourteen months old, I walked into my first therapy session since before having him. I was a bag of excruciating nerves. The therapist I'd been to before had retired and I'd never met this one before.

A therapist having therapy themselves is a strange thing until you get to know each other. *I know what you know, and I know you know, and you know I know.* You are looking at the session from so many different angles. By the time I had walked into the session, I was shaking like a leaf. I could fool those around me, I could hide postnatal depression from most people. But I knew full well that there is absolutely no point in therapy if you are going to try and hide stuff.

I had convinced myself that as soon as someone 'in the trade' knew how I was feeling; they would tell me to stop working immediately[27].

'What?! You are a counsellor? I'm reporting you! You are far too insane to do your job!' I imagined her saying.

Second only to damaging Wolfie, losing my identity as a therapist was my biggest fear. My work was the only solid thing in my life, the only thing I knew I was good at. If that was taken away, I would crumble. I was doing my best to parent, and thinking I was failing. Being back at work had made me feel like me again, and I couldn't lose that.

---

[27] I'll tell you a little secret. Therapists are human. Like me, a lot of therapists that I've met are a bit mad, and plenty of them make my little visit into madness look like a teddy bear's picnic. But of course the self-critical monster in my head seemed to conveniently forget this at the time, as it tried its best to bully me.

Thankfully, my therapist was shit hot. I felt the stress drain from my body as I got to know her. Unbeknown to me, she knew of me professionally and reassured me that whilst I was fighting my own demons, I was still more than capable of fighting the demons of my clients. She told me that she had heard that I was shit-hot at working with my clients. I cried when I heard that. She helped me understand that I hadn't lost the plot, that even though I had experienced poor mental health it didn't mean that I was a crap therapist.

My heart sang, I wasn't losing myself. In another session, she reminded me of an old saying from the therapy world that I had forgotten about.

'How do you regulate a therapist...?'

'Put a client in front of them.' [28]

How could I have forgotten that? Because it's true. A good therapist (and I like to think I'm a good therapist) leaves their shit at the door, and is wholly in their client's story when in session. So actually I'd been treating work like my sanctuary- in order to help my very vulnerable little clients, I had to leave my shit firmly at the door. But at the same time, leaving my shit at the door meant I could escape it. Becoming a workaholic was my rebellion against my shit. The more kids I helped the less I felt like there was no point to me. By the time Wolfgang was 10 months old, I was back to working full time, was a good chunk through a master's degree and had started a business. When I wasn't working, I was constantly thinking of ways I could be a better parent to Wolfgang. I was playing with him, helping him develop, making sure he felt as loved as any baby could ever feel, in a bid to make sure we did actually bond and that it was impossible for his mental health to be affected by mine. I was keeping myself busy doing what I knew how to do, instead of

---

[28] To 'regulate' means to help calm someone into a more stable state of mind.

175

spending time doing what I didn't know how to do, which was dealing with the monster in my own head.

My therapist helped me to understand all of this. Not only did she help me to understand that despite feeling like I was bat-shit bonkers, I was doing okay. Actually better than okay. It was as if she had helped me to turn a dial on a pair of binoculars. Things began to come into focus.

But I was wrong. She didn't. She didn't judge me at all. She explained to me that just because in one aspect of my life I was struggling, she could see that I was skilled and professional enough to continue doing the work I was doing. This was a huge turning point for me. I can't explain the relief. It was a really physical feeling like a wave of acceptance, my whole body flopped and I cried my eyes out. I had been carrying these feelings for literally years. What Wolfgang was doing, saving me from the abyss, my counsellor and the medication was helping. I was recovering and healing. My identity as a therapist wasn't lost, my reputation was intact (apart from the Jimmy Saville joke – I don't think there is any coming back from that).

The seed planted by my friends, my therapist nourished. I finally realised, *I didn't have to be perfect.*

41
Gin and Revelations

I was beginning to feel accepted. To accept myself. My self-acceptance was a bit awkward and clunky, but it was happening. My beautiful son, my soulmate Fernando, my friends, my family and my therapist accepted me, just as I was.

It was time to heal. The Scrummies really helped with that. They seemed to accept me, no questions asked, and most importantly accept the fact that we never met at my house. I was terrified for people to see it. I would always make some sort of excuse for why couldn't meet at mine, because I believed it to be too messy, which now I know was totally normal for a mum with a young baby. But at the time I felt like my house wasn't worthy and I couldn't cope with the thought of feeling any more shame after heaping so much of it onto my own head. I was slowly beginning to accept that I had something like postnatal depression, although I was still blaming myself for it.

At one gathering, I was talking about how exhausting I was finding it all. Chickenkicker listened closely to my troubles. She took a deep breath and began to tell me that she sometimes felt the same. She told me about one of her coping strategies. She had found a magical clear liquid. Drunk once a day at exactly 3pm would cure the madness, albeit temporarily.

It was gin. While I was sorely tempted to imbibe in her remedy, I didn't think I had the self-discipline to stop at one. I decided there and then that this was not for me; I couldn't fill my plate further with the added complication of becoming an alcoholic.

When Chickenkicker disclosed that, just to get through the day without losing the plot, she was having a secret gin at 3pm every day I could have wept in joy, I really could. Not at her struggles of course, but because it meant that somebody else was finding it outrageously hard too. I had found more others like me. We Scrummies had begun to find each other.

Infrequent and tiny little starbursts of clarity came to me, and I began to understand that everyone was winging it somehow. Whether it's pretending that you don't miss your old life, or crying with frustration as you're furiously wet wiping sick off your only clean pair of trousers, or having a secret gin every afternoon just to help you get through the day. We all had to step up to an invisible mark when we became new mothers, except nobody told us where the bloody mark was, and we just couldn't find it.

Being with the Scrummies saved my sanity. Side-splitting, pig-snorting, coffee-spilling hilarity and genuineness and a comfortable space of vulnerability between us. Pubwatch is the sort of person who makes you believe that you can do absolutely anything. After I spend time with her, I think can take on the world.

Excuse my fanciful metaphors, but I believe that a woman becoming a mother is like raw metal becoming a sword. You need to melt, shape, mould and strengthen yourself. Change your raw materials into whatever your baby needs. Doing this while suffering with postnatal depression is like doing all that and then some; tempering your steel with fire, burning yourself again and again and again.

After the first few months of utter hell, I had made this important discovery. I wasn't the only one. I wasn't the *only* other… there were *other* others. We were all struggling with something. I haven't been lucky enough to experience new motherhood without the Brucie Bonus of having postnatal depression. But from what I can gather when I talk to the Scrummies, this experience of becoming a mother thing is a bit of a spectrum. No two experiences are the same, even for the same mother who has more than one child. It's not a case of either being a completely perfect or a completely mental mother. I haven't met anyone who really and truly didn't struggle with anything. Which means that maybe even those bloody Yummies struggled, even if they did it in perfect cropped pants with amazing messy buns.

I'm not a big fan of the word sisterhood. Don't get me wrong I like the concept very much, but the word conjures up twee images of nuns and WI market stalls for some reason. And to a nun I most certainly cannot be compared. Baby Lunatics like me, Scrummies like my wonderful friends, are real. Laughing, sharing, swearing and reaching out a hand to pull each other out of the shit.

Wolfgang is still friends with the kids of the Scrummies. He and Sleepless Beauty's youngest, Beastie, are now inseparable. Like a pair of feral superheroes, they constantly fight to ensure that neither of them becomes the sidekick. They love each other to bits and it's really cute to watch them. Just the other day they were muddy in the river in their underpants, fighting with sticks while some of our more sensible friends had their kids geared up for the occasion in their water shoes and wetsuits. I still cringe when other people's kids behave so politely and wouldn't dream of fighting with a stick, but now I do it with a laugh and a giggle outwardly, not an abusive internal assault on myself. Because my real friends, the Scrummies, taught me that it was okay for things to be a bit shit. For me to be a bit mental and for Wolfgang to be a bit feral. That we were doing just fine. They don't know this, but their support probably helped me to avoid feeling the need to wobble that steering wheel towards that huge drop anymore. The more they accepted and embraced me, the more I could accept that I'd had some sort of breakdown, some sort of postnatal mental health issue.

I was accepting that the culpability for the shit hitting the fan inside my brain probably lay with my hormones, rather than some failure on my part as a mother, as a person.

PART THREE

42
Big Girl Knickers

Time marched on, as it does. I was getting better every day, but I was still terrified of people judging us and I was still worrying constantly that I had damaged my beautiful Wolfgang. In fact, I'm not sure if that worry will ever disappear absolutely. My feelings that my son would be better off without me were constant companions for about a year after he was born, returned regularly during the second year and dramatically diminished during the third year. But in between these periods of madness, something good was happening. Something in me was fighting back, and in those times I got glimpses of who I really was, and sometimes, I wasn't a shit mother. I was a mother whose mental health was a bit shit.

The first time my maternal inner she-wolf really came out, I was startled. Wolfgang was four months old and we were on a family holiday to Cornwall with Hosenose and her family, The Criminal Mastermind and our parents Sunshine and Slipalong (kindly tolerating each other so we could have a family holiday).

Something happened on this holiday which I will never forget... and it was real. And just for a moment postnatal depression was completely obliterated by my animalistic need to protect him. It was the first time I felt like an authentic and indisputable mother. For a few seconds I was wholly Wolfgang's Mam. Not mad, not sad, not perfect but damn near close. He had been born around 160 days previously, 160 days of hating myself and thinking awful thoughts. *I just didn't have it in me to be a decent mother.*

As a family we were about to board a small cruise boat for some trip, I forget now what it was all about, and Fernando was carrying Wolfgang in his car seat. We had to walk down a steep set of stairs off a high jetty in order to get on the boat. Fernando is an incredibly strong, big bloke and would never ever have dropped Wolfgang, but just for a split second, as he was carrying Wolfgang down the narrow steps, there was nothing but air between Wolfie in his car seat and the churning sea, about ten feet below us.

In that moment, I thought he was going to drop my baby. I went fucking ape shit. I think that's the day when I realised that I was a mother, and that day, a little tigress was born in my head, a little she-wolf who would soon grow bigger and stronger than the poor postnatal-diseased creature who also lived inside. Fernando got a mouthful of abuse and I grabbed the car seat from his hands. Okay, I was that fucking angry I almost pushed Fernando in the water. It took me hours to calm down after that. Fernando has very mixed feelings about this day. Probably because he couldn't see inside my head. I had behaved like a lunatic, screaming at him about something he hadn't done, then grinning all afternoon, because I realised something, *I bloody did have it in me to be a decent mother.*

There's a cool photo of me holding Wolfgang on that boat. I was smiling like a Cheshire cat because I finally felt it. I'd actually *felt* it. Those photographs are really important to me now. Especially those of my early days with Wolfgang. As I sit here and write this I am looking at another photo of us, this one from the day after my boy was born. Initially I hated this photograph. All I could see was my death-like make-up-free face and remember when the photograph was taken. The weight of my son pressed on my chest like the weight of the world. The weight of that tiny boy was immense, representing to me the weight I would now carry for the rest of my life, weight not really caused by Wolfgang, but by my mental health. I nearly sank.

Now I can not only appreciate that there was actually beauty in me as a new mother, but also my son's gorgeous little round head, the curled fingers and the face snuggled into my chest. I couldn't feel the love then; it was blocked out by the trauma of his birth. But I do now. I feel blessed to have this photograph. Because now I feel it, now I feel it like a mother. I feel it so much it brings tears to my eyes, especially when I admit to myself that I can't remember most of my son's first year. It cuts deeply that I only felt pain and I guess my mind's response was to forget, to shut down. But deep down, my memories must have survived because even though I wasn't there at the time, I can be there now. I wonder if you are still there reader, or whether my nonsensical bull-shitty ramblings have caused you to stick this book in the recycling bin.

I wish I could tell you that parenting gets easier. It did for me but not until Wolfgang would be about five years old. I don't know if it's the same for everyone or whether it was just me, but even as the monster of postnatal was dying, I was still overwhelmed by being a parent. Maybe it was because of the postnatal depression that it took me longer to settle into the role?

I don't know, I was under an awful lot of pressure as well I guess, pressure that I helpfully insisted on heaping upon myself. In my usual fashion, I decided to start a Master's degree when Wolfie was twelve weeks old. Probably another attempt to make myself feel worthy. How I scraped that qualification with being a new parent and having mental health issues I'll never know. I had to change the subject of my research of course. Living through postnatal depression and studying it at the same time would have blown my head straight off my shoulders. It was utter madness. I was working four days a week, trying to set up

183

my own business and complete my MA. Thankfully Fernando and I have great mothers, they helped a lot with childcare.

I seemed to be always moving, driving backwards and forwards, on my computer, feeding the baby, changing nappies, answering emails, typing long into the night, looking at the clock wondering if I had time for an hour's sleep before Wolfie woke for a feed, every minute of every day.

But there was one thing even I couldn't fuck up. Cuddles. Touch and emotional engagement are crucial for developing babies. It helps them to regulate their temperature, heart rate and breathing. It soothes the baby and increases both the mother and baby's relaxation hormones, and WorkHead knew all about this. HomeHead must've been listening, because, blimey I cuddled that baby, and I think one of the special things that saved us was the sheer amount of cuddles we had. After he was about six months old, at afternoon nap time, I would ritually cuddle him, sitting in my bed and would stare at him for a couple of hours after he had fallen asleep, despite all the other things I had to do. It was like a lovely pause in my mad rollercoaster.

In the early days of doing this I used to silently berate myself for wasting time. I should have been cleaning, tidying, studying and all the other things that needed to be done. But for some reason, perhaps my instincts were finally winning, as I chose to spend that couple of hours every day holding him while he slept. He was gorgeous, I used to smell the top of his head, rest with him and something was telling me to hold him, hold him, hold him.

I beat myself up for it though, my stupid mind was torturing me again, rewarding me with more crushing anxiety that I was also a shit mother for doing this. For staying with him, when I wasn't needed (he would be asleep) and that I should be downstairs cleaning. I hate that anxiety ruined even that for me.

But something was changing, and I don't know how, but sometimes I was able to ignore that screaming voice that called me *lazy*. Something was telling me to stay just there, quite often in stained pyjamas, clutching him to me in an unmade bed, whilst he slumbered in my arms, clean as a whistle in a sparkling baby-grow.

I truly believe that helped us massively to bond. My true self was waking up, determined to fight this. I think my instincts were telling me to hold him, and hold him, and hold him, even if my stupid brain was telling me to wash the dishes. This wasn't meant as any sort of how-to book, but if I can give any advice to anyone feeling the same, listen to your arms wanting to stay where they are and the peaceful snore of your baby. Bollocks to the washing up.

43
Your Bloody Father!

I was getting better, but mad shit kept happening. Returning to work after maternity leave, I still led a double life for a long time. In work I was being treated as if I knew what I was talking about, but my personal life was still a shit show at times. I was still like a magnet for chaos, even more than before I became pregnant with Wolfie. The shit that happened to me didn't seem to happen to anyone else!

'I haven't got fucking time for this. He's a fucking tit. I can't believe this. It's a fucking joke!' I raged as I flew in through Hosenose's door, still in my suit and high heels from work.

'What's up?' she asked.

'Can you look after Wolfgang?' I asked, throwing the nappy bag and almost throwing 10-month-old Wolfgang to her, strapped into his car seat.

'I have to go and pick Fernando up from fucking A and E. He's fucking gone and fainted or something at the dentist! Apparently the dentist was a big guy and was doing CPR on him. I don't fucking know what's happened.'

I'd been delivering a training day on mental health.

Ha! If the participants on the training only knew!

About an hour before the end of the training day I'd glimpsed at my phone to check that I was delivering the training to the right timescale. I had nine missed calls from Fernando. I handed over to my co-trainer and slipped out of the training room to call him back and see what on earth had made him call me nine times.

'Don't panic…' *Cue instant panic.* 'But I'm in Accident and Emergency. I had to have CPR at the dentist.'

'You fucking what? Are you okay?? What the hell? Oh my god, are you alright?'

186

'Yeah. I'm fine. They had to do CPR on me, then I had to come to hospital to check that they hadn't broken any of my ribs. Can you come and pick me up?'

'Why did they have to do CPR on you??'

'Because I died in the dentist's chair.'

'You what? You fucking died?!?!'

'Well they think now I fainted and they couldn't find my pulse.' I could hear the embarrassment in his voice.

'So you didn't actually die?'

'No.'

'So…... you just fainted.'

'Yes.'

'Right... I'll be there as soon as I can. I'll have to get Wolfgang from the childminders, drop him off with Hosenose and I'll be there'.

I couldn't fucking believe what I'd just been told.

Apparently, as soon as he had had the numbing injection in his gum, his eyes had rolled into the back of his head and he had flopped back into the chair. He told me that he remembers he was having a lovely dream, when he heard panicked, echo-like shouts.

'Mr Fernando!? *Mr Fernando*!?'

He came round, feeling rested after a deep sleep.

Oh shit. I'm not in bed. I'm at the dentist, he thought to himself.

Fernando opened his eyes to see two of the dental nurses sobbing as if they were already at his funeral. They must have thought that Fernando truly was dead. The next minute, he felt like he was being stepped on by an elephant as the dentist began pumping away at his chest, convinced that Fernando was a goner. Apparently, they had been unable to find a pulse after Fernando's eyes rolled back into his head – he has skin like a rhinoceros so I'm not surprised.

Apparently it was fucking pandemonium in the clinic.

You need to know something important here. Unless someone's heart has actually stopped beating, performing CPR on them is very dangerous. Because of George the Dentist and his over-enthusiastic attempts at first aid, Fernando had to be checked out by a paramedic to ensure that his heart was beating normally and hadn't been knocked out of rhythm. Bless him, an ambulance was called, and when they informed him that he had to actually go to hospital he protested strongly that he had to get back to work. He was determined that he wasn't going to hospital. But apparently, he fainted again in the ambulance whilst the paramedic was checking him over. The paramedic who was a tiny - but clearly resourceful- woman, took her opportunity and buckled him into the gurney so well that when he came round he was stuck. She then shouted 'Go!' to the driver and off they sped to hospital, Fernando trussed up and severely pissed off.

He still tells people that he died in the dentist's chair.

Somehow, I had the leftovers of postnatal depression, mad shit like this would happen and send my anxiety soaring, and work were still expecting me to do a sterling job. I had begun to think that I was destined for madness and not greatness. Before I left work for maternity leave, I was beginning to write academic articles, sometimes even teaching other people about it, infant mental health, children's mental health, maternal mental health.

Then when I returned to work, they started asking again... and I felt like the biggest fraud who ever walked the Earth. It really turned the screw tighter on my secret agony.

It…

Was…

Fucking…

Crippling.

Like Alice, I'd passed through a mirror, and everything I thought I knew just wasn't quite right. The substance of everything had changed, but to everyone else, it looked exactly the same. Worse than that, I was supposed to be Lewis Carroll, the author of my baby's mental health journey (as all mothers are) but really, deep down inside I was more like the Mad Hatter. I felt that I was orchestrating the destruction of his mental health before I had the chance to help create it. Yet in work, my colleagues were treating me like some sort of expert. I was being paid to help children and young people, and simultaneously I felt like I was damaging my own.

It wasn't just the confusion and horror of actually experiencing postnatal depression, it was doubly hard because of the guilt and fear of what could happen to Wolfgang because of what I thought was my weakness, of what I believed was my unnatural response to having a baby. I knew exactly what could happen. I knew attachment, child development theory and the neurodevelopment of babies' brains inside out. Working in mental health where it was expected that I knew what I was doing made it triply hard. I'm not sure if *Triply* is actually a word as it happens, but you know what I mean.

My experiences as a mother meant that I'd been feeling like a fraud both at home and in work, when I'd first returned from maternity leave. But I had to get on with it. I had no choice, I had to find a way through it all. I began to find the confidence and belief I used to have in myself in work, and I began build some confidence in myself as a mother, in my new role.

This was my new normal. My big girl pants started fitting me again (obviously I mean that metaphorically, there's no way I was getting back into my pre-Wolfie pants yet).

I was managing to get back into the swing of things in work, and I made it work at home. Thankfully, Wolfgang developed normally and he grew fast. He was hitting all his developmental milestones; he was growing appropriately and had lost any resemblance to Tweetie Pie. In fact, he was always quick for his age, especially when it came to language, I would find to my cost.

And suddenly….. he was a toddler. I would just start to relax, thinking everything was going to be okay, but I was hyperalert for signs that I had damaged him with postnatal depression. It would all be going great and then things like this would happen and my mind would spiral

Uh oh. There it is. I did damage him.

'Mam!!!!! There he is!!!! There's my bloody Father!!!!!'

Wolfgang was almost two years old when he shouted this at the top of his voice… in public[29]. Again in fucking Gossip & Groceries. The Psycho Woman's kid was swearing at the top of his voice, pointing up the alcohol aisle.

Fernando is fucking useless at food shopping. In fact, he's worse than useless. He either wanders off up the music and entertainment aisle and I can't find him, or he just fills my basket with cookies and beer. My shopping bill is always higher when he comes with me. It's like having a 6-foot toddler in tow. On this particular day I'd lost my marbles a bit at his wanderings and muttered under my breath.

---

[29] The only other time I can remember being this embarrassed was in a shop one time in a bakery. The lady behind the counter asked me what I would like to order. 'One chocolate lesbian please', I replied, and for a couple of seconds I smiled at her. I meant to ask for a chocolate éclair. I had just been talking to my friend in the queue about equal rights, and my brain must have malfunctioned. After a garbled incoherent explanation and a red-faced apology, I grabbed my chocolate lesbian and fled from there too, leaving my friend who was doubled over crying with laughter.

'Where's your bloody father gone now'?

It could have been worse. Thankfully, he didn't add the 'for fuck's sake' I had also uttered, to the 'Mam! There's my bloody Father…'

A year later, it was nearly Christmas, and we were again in the famous Gossip & Groceries. All of a sudden, Wolfgang started screeching.

'Mam! Look at that fat ginger man!' at the top of his voice.

I looked to where he was pointing and there was indeed a tall, 'well-built' red-haired man standing about six feet away from us in the aisle. The guy turned round and I carefully looked everywhere but at his face. Cringing horribly, I happened to look up. Above the guy's head there hung a massive gingerbread man – you know the hanging cardboard type of thing they use for advertising at Christmas?

'Yes baby, it is a massive gingerBREAD man, isn't it?' I replied at the top of my voice. I swiftly turned the trolley around and fled.

In my new role as a parent to a toddler, I was like an incompetent health and safety officer, constantly trying and often failing in my risk assessments of every part of every little thing in his little life. As well as swearing in Gossip & Groceries and insulting people, one of Wolfgang's hobbies when he was around three was collecting Blu Tac. He was a Blu Tac connoisseur. I used to find globs of the bloody stuff stuck all over the house. I shit you not, he used to find it everywhere. If there was Blu Tac to be found in the vicinity, Wolfgang would find it. I have seen him with a blob of Blu Tac in his hand hundreds of times, but I have never once caught him peeling it off walls.

Therefore, one day, I couldn't understand why my dad was heaving and pointing at Wolfgang who was playing with another lump of it. We'd just come out of a hospital where we'd

191

been visiting a friend so I presumed he had found some on the wall and nicked it. Slipalong was trying to say something to me in between retching.

'That's not bloody Blu Tac! It's old chewing gum!'

Fuck…

Around the same time, Wolfgang, like lots of children, developed a fascination with his bum. I remember once I'd been running round like a blue-arsed fly, trying to get us out of the house on time and looking presentable when Wolfie proudly made an announcement.

'Mam. I've just stuck my finger right inside my bum.'

To my shame, I just rubbed his finger with a wet wipe and replied in a singsong voice.

'*Annnnd* we are going to just pretend you never said that.'

Off we went to the party.

It wasn't just his actual bum he was
fascinated with either. It was the word Bum.

'Hah ha Mam. Buuuuuum in the face!' He attacks me by sitting on my head, or reversing up to me squatting.

'Buuuuuuum, Buuuuuuuum, Buuuuuuum!' he used to try out the word in different accents (yes, my child can do accents), his favourite is a gravelly pirate's voice. His second favourite is a highland Scottish accent. I know this because it is ingrained in my bloody brain. I feel as though not a single human on the planet has heard the word *bum* as many times as I have.

We were walking through a posh food market in York. We were there on holiday and it was a quiet, sunny day. All of a sudden Wolfie piped up.

'You got blood on your face, you big disgrace, waving your bum all over the place' to the famous Queen song. A couple of stallholders and passers-by all chuckled and thought it was cute. I cringed because I suspected what might be coming next…

and encouraged by his audience (Wolfie loves an audience) he belted out the next line to his song.

'We will, we will bum you. Sing it… we will, we will bum you!!!!'

The smiles on the faces of the stall holders and the other tourists froze and their eyes widened. Fernando, seeing my face, clutched me and Wolfgang by the shoulders and steered us into the nearest pub, and ordered me a huge glass of wine. He knows how stuff like this can send me spiralling. However, nobody knew us there and after I had drank about half the wine, I started laughing and couldn't stop, as Wolfie continued to sing his song to a thankfully empty pub, and the more I laughed, the louder he sang…

44
Another Brick in the Wall

Unfortunately, when he was three-and-a-half there was something else over the horizon that was going to make me wobble a bit again. Sigh. I probably should have saved this bit for the second book, if anyone is mad enough to buy the first one! So the Baby Lunatic turned into the Kid Lunatic I guess. The mad shit didn't stop as soon as I recovered from postnatal depression. It wasn't a cut and dried thing. I didn't just recover then everything was normal. Being a mum to a young child, when you have the left-over gifts of having experienced postnatal depression, isn't easy either. The huge issue that was looming over our heads was that Wolfgang was about to start school, and the thought of him starting school terrified me.

Just when I thought I had this thing nailed, calmed this anxiety and begun to believe a little that that I hadn't somehow damaged Wolfie, something else came along and bit me on the arse to remind me that this motherhood thing was never going to be easy.

My just-out-of-nappies baby, was just beginning to show me that everything was okay. I'd pretty much missed the first year, almost two, in a haze of terrified anxiety and now he was being sucked into the machine of education.

I bought him his tiny little school uniform, he was registered and accepted to the local primary. It was the primary school that I'd been to, never really a happy place for me, and I think this made me worry too. I was sending him out into the big wide world when he couldn't even wipe his own bum.

On our first day, parents were invited to stay with their children for the session. So we walked in, hand in hand, looked at where his little peg was, took his little coat off and walked into the classroom. A teacher came to meet us. She didn't appear very kind and she didn't really smile. My heart sank. I had to leave my baby with this woman, in a sea of thirty other babies.

My boy needed warmth and smiles and to be nurtured in school, and I really needed him to be cared for properly.

My mind began to spiral.

Argh no, I can't leave him here. I want to take him home. Argh no. I can't I can't I can't. All this was going on in my head before she had even said a word. I was in bits inside. Smiling and chatting politely to the other mums on the outside.

We were introduced to the teaching assistants. Holy mother of God. It was her... Miss Trunchbull. The same evil-miserable-bitch-teaching-assistant that had been in the school when I was there. I was thirty-four years old for god's sake. How was it even possible? She hadn't aged a fucking day, and I decided there and then she must be some sort of robot. When I was at school, Miss Trunchbull was the scariest creature in the whole world. She was the one who would tell me off constantly and disapprove when I needed the toilet. She never smiled or laughed. Basically, she made me feel like shit as a child, her scratchy nails rustling through my hair, enthusiastically looking for nits.

And now, I had to leave my child in the same class as that woman. No fucking way. Miss Trunchbull was not going to do that to my child. I'd snap her fingers off if she tried to check Wolfie's hair. I would. I fucking would.

Inside I was in total pieces while chatting politely to the robot about how lovely it was that she had taught me and now would be teaching Wolfgang!

Somehow I did it. I took him there for three hours a day. He usually came home with a sore bum and a full lunchbox. It drove me mad how he would come home and nobody had helped him wipe his bottom at nursery or encouraged him to eat any of his lunch. His poor little arms couldn't even reach around properly to wipe his bottom. I felt so sorry for him and yet again utterly powerless. Powerlessness for me equals poor mental health we all know what happens now don't we.

Wolfgang often talked about how he had been told off by Miss Trunchbull for not sitting on the mat. I worried a little about this but thought I had no choice and would just have to see how it went. I suppose I was terrified of confronting the teacher and Miss Trunchbull as well and so I didn't bring it up with them.

At the end of that first term, I began to slip back down the rabbit hole of anxiety. It was again about power and control I think and my memories of Miss Trunchbull, Wolfgang's poor little sore bum from the neglect at school – yes it was neglect, it really was – and how hungry he was after school. But the final push into the rabbit hole was the class's first little concert.

Fernando and I both took the day off for this momentous occasion. Our boy's first ever concert. It was held in the classroom and we filed in with all the other parents smiling benevolently at the other parents and the children, beaming when we looked towards an excitedly waving little Wolfgang.

The singing began. Each child sat carefully cross-legged on their little individual mat. I winked at Wolfgang who calmly smiled at me, his eyes full of pride and purpose. The piano began to play and the children started singing. All of them... except Wolfgang.

Wolfgang got up off his mat and turned into the crazy frog. The savage little beast proceeded to run around the rest of the children playing knock and run on their heads. He must have hurt quite a few of them and the cute little singing was punctuated by the multiple screeches of 'Ow!' as he made his way around the other kids. Gradually this turned into stereo snivelling. Round and round the other kids he flew, my face of thunder and gritted teeth having no effect on him whatsoever. Miss Trunchbull was unable to catch him as he was so nimble weaving in and out of the other children, who were all siting nicely on their mats. Should I intervene? I didn't know what on earth to do.

All of them sat on their bloody mats. All of them apart from my barbaric little swine. And there it was… the evidence of the damage that I had inflicted on him. Me. I had done this. By the time Fernando and I had driven home from the concert – me in tears the whole time - I had diagnosed[30] him with ADHD, ODD, Attachment Disorder and a whole host of other behavioural problems. And it was all my fault. All of it.

Of course it wasn't my fault. Of course there were other children running around like savages. But I couldn't see them. Thankfully, nowadays he behaves perfectly in school. Since that first year in school he has had a new teacher. We shall call her Miss Honey. Miss Honey is lovely and a wonderful teacher. Miss Honey, we love you in our house. Wolfgang has flourished under your guidance.

Miss Honey helped me to climb out of the rabbit hole, and she doesn't even know it. She treated my little savage as a wonderful, interesting curious little boy and under her influence that's what he has become. Miss Trunchbull never did check my son for nits with her scratchy nails, as far as I know, and to this day she continues to work with the nursery class. God help them.

---

[30] Although I work with all sorts of conditions, syndromes and disorders, I am not technically trained or qualified to diagnose anyone with anything. Just so you know.

45

On the Red

There's a traffic light system for behaviour management in our school. On the Friday of Wolfie's first week in reception with Miss Honey, I was waiting for him outside his class. One of the boys who came out before him smiled at me with a massive grin and told me the gossip, in an annoying and unnecessarily loud sing-song voice.

'Wolfgang is on the Red!'

Being 'on the Red' is the ultimate shame and proof of naughtiness at this primary school. If your name ever gets put on the Red, it seems that you are royally fucked… prison here we come. Neither my niece nor nephew had ever been on the Red, ever. At all. And here was Wolfgang, on the Red in his first week.

I remember feeling like I was going to die with shame, it was a big deal at the time. I can't remember now what heinous crime he had committed this time, but I do remember however, the second time he was put on the Red was in Year 2. Between Nursery and Year 2, we (I say we because I was so paranoid about it that I was right there with him on that red circle of shame) had only been on the Orange occasionally. I could cope with the occasional misdemeanours that led to us being on Orange.

But in Year 2, while waiting for him outside his class at the end of the day, I was asked to come in for a chat with his teacher.

'May I have a word Mrs Baby Lunatic? It's a very serious matter I'm afraid.'

The edges of my vision closed in with instant anxiety. What the fuck? My mind whirled! *What on earth could he have done, aged five, to warrant it being called a very serious matter?* Had he maimed another child? Had he bitten the head teacher? Had he robbed the secretary's petty cash tin? Had he stabbed Miss Trunchbull in the eye with a pencil?? *What on earth had he done?!*

I followed the teacher into the classroom and to my relief walked in to see two other parents, dads perched on tiny chairs, squirming and looking uncomfortable. Thankfully, one of them was Beastie's dad (Sleepless Beauty's partner who I've known forever) and the other was another friendly father whose son was friends with Wolfgang. It turned out that the three little gits had discovered a pile of stones and started lobbing them at each other. Throwing stones and pretending they were weapons. Thankfully I had a bit of a laugh about it with the two dads after we had been in for this chat and got over the trauma. Our three kids were subsequently banned from playing Power Rangers in school ever again.

Every parent's evening, I wait outside for my turn to meet the teacher, shaking like a shitting dog. I perch on one of those tiny little benches, my gut wrenching with fear in case they suddenly start saying there is something wrong with Wolfgang. It's totally irrational I know. He's a great little dude, and he's thankfully thriving under Miss Honey.

God forbid he comes home and says he's had a fight with one of the other kids at school. I imagine the worst and expect some furious mother to karate chop my confidence by asking me for that most terrifying thing, a word. Other people's judgement still scares the shit out of me.

46
Feral?

Talking about other people's judgement… On holiday when he was four he ran towards me, soaking wet and skidding towards my sun lounger, and almost knocked my mojito over, the little sod.

'Hi Mam! I'm feral!' he shouted at me and leapt sideways into the swimming pool like some sort of deranged salmon.

Without… his… fucking… armbands!

At the point I was about to jump in to rescue him, Fernando realised that his charge had escaped and that our son was effectively and gleefully drowning. Spluttering from the tsunami splash of Fernando diving in to save Wolfgang, I breathed a sigh of relief that he had once again avoided certain death. The grip of anxiety about his safety still had a lump of postnatal depression hidden in the middle of it and poor Fernando got it in the neck for taking his eyes off Wolfgang. I also still shudder at the possibilities of what misdemeanour he must have committed in order for someone to refer to him as feral. He was clever, but he wasn't that bloody clever. Someone had definitely called him FERAL.

I know that Wolfgang's godmother, The Enforcer, also thinks he's a bit feral, but then she has known me for decades, and given how feral she knows me to be, I think she thinks he's doing okay. I think The Enforcer is the only person that Wolfgang is actually scared of. Children *do not* fuck with The Enforcer. She's a wonderful disciplinarian. I remember once that Wolfgang had put a marble in his mouth. A muddy, germ ridden marble that he had found on the floor. I couldn't get it out of his mouth for love nor money and I was worried sick he was going to swallow or choke on it. He had had the marble in his mouth for about fifteen minutes by now. Fortune was shining on us because the next minute The Enforcer walked into my house. Wide eyed, Wolfgang eyes flicked between me and The Enforcer as I explained what was going on, Wolfgang knew what was going to happen, his lips clamped shut, like a hamster with booty in his cheeks, he tried to back away from us.

'Out!' was all she said. The marble plopped into her cupped hand. She's a brilliant godmother. Takes no shit. I don't know how she does it. As well as being able to make kids behave with just a glance of an eye, The Enforcer also is one of the only people who can tell when there is something wrong with me. Immediately, before I have even opened my mouth. If I didn't know her so well I would be worried by the creepy way in which she does this. She just knows. Is she psychic? Is she a stalker? She has marvellous eyebrows and I'm jealous of those eyebrows. The Enforcer somehow, just by breathing, makes you feel like you are coming home. She makes you feel safe... and sometimes scared, because she's a tiny bit bossy.

47

Hmmm… Which one of us is Feral?

Life was getting much better, I was beginning to accept that I was okay, that I could somehow do this thing, spin the plates of work and home, and do my best. It was hard, and lonely sometimes, sometimes still slightly feeling like I was leading a double life, but it was okay, I was managing. I was becoming slightly less crackers. We were doing okay, most of the time. The lunacy that accompanied Wolfgang's birth hadn't entirely left me, but by revealing how I had been feeling to the Scrummies, I was healing.

Don't get me wrong, the madness of trying to be at certain places at certain times drove me insane. I was doing my very best with trying to be the world's most effective children's therapist and at the same time the world's best mother. The plates were bound to come crashing down around my ears occasionally, at which point I would do something really stupid or occasionally, I used to deal with my stress by getting spectacularly shitfaced.

When Wolfgang was four years old (not long after the Feral incident), I was invited to The Enforcer's hen weekend abroad. This was a huge test for me. By now, I was almost fine. I say 'almost' because there was an element of guilt and worry, that my illness had affected him. Work was mental (there's a pun in there somewhere) and I was working 50-60 hour weeks. Something was about to give. My dignity and sobriety were hanging by a thread.

One part of me couldn't wait for the hen do, I was so excited, but at the same time, leaving Wolfgang in a different country even with Fernando (despite trusting him implicitly) brought some anxieties back. So by the time we got to the airport I was reeling after weeks of non-stop working and anxious about leaving Wolfie. I began to deal with this stress by ordering a massive glass of wine at the airport. Over the next 24 hours I drank enough alcohol that I should have permanently damaged myself.

I had fled the stress of work, I wasn't having to concentrate so intently on keeping together the mind and body of a young child. I didn't need to be a Health and Safety Officer for a few days. In fact, looking back at my behaviour, it was me who needed a Health and Safety Officer.

Thank the lord, I did indeed have my own personal Health and Safety Officer, because Hosenose was also a bridesmaid.

It was a good job she was. Because I got absolutely shitfaced.

Oh.....to be in a different country, to be free, to be in the warm sunshine and to feel young again. It was my first time away from home on a girls' thing since having Wolfie. I drank way, way too many shots in my haste to abandon everyday life. We all got dressed in matching dresses with pink sashes, and I plopped the massive pink penis boppers on my head, before downing yet another jagerbomb whilst we did our make-up. Hosenose looked on, a wary smile on her face. She bloody knew, didn't she.

The hen do challenges involved having my chest autographed and claiming random bits of men's clothing in a bar. I was determined, I won most of the challenges, so even more shots were flying my way.

Hosenose began to notice how much more-drunk-than-everyone-else I was becoming. It was getting late. Despite my pissed protests, she insisted that it was time we went back to the hotel. Dragging me out of the club we were in, she ended up having a massive argument with a Spanish taxi driver who had to be begged to allow me in his taxi. He was worried that I would vomit all over his taxi, and his concerns weren't misplaced. I got back to the apartment and was looked after by The Enforcer (the bride) who held back my hair as I chunged up like a 1990's teenager who had sunk too much Mad Dog 20/20. Fair play to her, she wasn't angry at all about it. I think I am so responsible most of the time that she found it amusing, maybe not at the time, but afterwards.

It gets worse. I was sharing a room with Hosenose, who although being the younger sister, (who may I add once attacked me with a vodka bottle, but Sunshine says I'm not allowed to talk about that) is much more sensible than I am.

Remember my sleepwalking? Alcohol makes it worse. Hosenose, knows this. So in order to stop her older, pissed up, sleepwalking sister coming to any harm by wandering around sleepwalking and pissed out of her mind in a foreign country, she had barricaded the patio door to stop me escaping. But she couldn't tie me to the bed.

Having chunged my guts up and crawled into bed, she waited up for a while to make sure I didn't chung again and choke to death (she is a much better sister than I am). Disgusted at me, she had dragged her bed as far across the room as she could from the snoring, stinking mess that was me on the other side of the room. Apparently, just as she was drifting off, I frightened her, because suddenly I got up, changed into my pyjamas, walked into the bathroom and layered on about half an inch of face cream. Face creamed up, apparently I began wandering around our apartment flicking lights on and off, looking at Hosenose and in a sing-song voice saying: 'Fuck off, fuck off, fuck off!' with each click, over and over.

Needless to say I was in the doghouse the following morning. I wonder what a dream interpreter would make of my shenanigans?

Thankfully, I didn't choke on my own vomit, and Hosenose didn't kill me. The Enforcer loves me enough to forgive my outrageous behaviour (I was bloody chief bridesmaid and everything, crrrrriiinnngggeeee). I am so lucky that I have a group of special friends who I can be my own idiotic self around.

My friends laugh rather than judge at the outrageous things that I sometimes do, and things that still come out of my mouth sometimes. My jokes are not as insulting or as jaw-droppingly inappropriate now, but I do open my gob and the maddest shit comes out.

The second night of the hen do, Hosenose and I had had a glass of wine (it was all I could stomach) and were having an early night. We spent the next couple of hours sharing a bottle of wine and talking, between the demands of our respective family members, we didn't often get time to chat like this.

After we had turned off the lights and were in bed. She had deigned to move her bed back to its proper place.

'You are better now, aren't you?', she said.

It was very cathartic to hear her say it. It was the first time ether of us had properly acknowledged how ill I'd been with postnatal depression, and how much of a journey I'd been on.

Very charitably, The Enforcer and Hosenose forgave me. I think I was forgiven so quickly because they knew how hard the last few years had been, very few people did know. I slowly began to forgive myself as well.

I had spent the last few years torturing myself in this post-natal depression hell, denial stopping me from seeking the help that I needed, the help I knew how to give, but not how to receive. Eventually I broke down to my doctor about it and I was fortunate to get the help I needed. Eventually I was put on Prozac to help with anxiety and continued seeing my wonderful counsellor.

The message was getting through to my brain. The message that..

... Sometimes mothers and therapists might lose their shit but can still do both their jobs properly...

...was so, so powerful.

I was going to be okay, I was even beginning to believe that Wolfgang was going to be okay, and that I hadn't harmed his fragile precious infant development. I'd protected him from the monster. He hadn't been harmed. Everything was going to be okay.

48
All the way home

'Wolfgang? I said.

'Yes Mami?' he replied, smiling a gummy smile at me.

'Wolfgang, I love you all the way round the world, shooting through the stars, loop the loop round the moon and all the way up to the sun.'

'And Mami? I love you all the way home.'

The day he replied unprompted with that was the day I felt fully recovered. He was three years, four months, and twelve days old. I felt like I had melted, the wind knocked out of me in a good way. It was so unexpected. I used to say the first line to him all the time and when he replied with that off his own back, it felt like the click of a padlock. This important but broken padlock, which had never closed properly, which had never been safe, had finally clicked into place and was secure.

Wolfgang held the key.

I remember Sleepless Beauty once told me that the bond between a mother and her child is stronger than even the closest romantic relationship; you kind of make your own little soulmate. I didn't understand that back when she told me.

Now I do. Because after conquering postnatal depression, and considering our bond so carefully, now I do. I absolutely adore my little Wolfgang, and if I had to go through all that madness and mental illness in order to have him again. I would. I would a hundred times.

I honestly never thought it would happen, that this stranger child and the body I was living in would actually become real and bonded. I can only describe the bond with your child as falling in love. For most people this happens straight after birth. But for me, it was built bit by bit as the depression began to clear. It was painful and seemed impossible; it was like wading through treacle. I was taught young that you have to pull yourself up by the bootstraps. I'm used to pulling myself up by the bootstraps, except this time I didn't even have any fucking boots on.

But we did bond, he was no longer a stranger to me, and the mother in me was no longer a stranger to me either. Pretence became reality and the magic happened. With every kiss I gave my son, with every cuddle, every song I sang him and later every push of the swing, I kept us safe from the darkest places, I clung on and saved us both from falling into the abyss of my mind.

In a strange way, I count myself lucky now that we went through all this. Blessed with an incredible closeness with my son, as the falling in love with him happened over a longer period of time. Maybe it is even more special than a typical mother-child bond, maybe because I fought harder for it. I walked through hell for that bond, now I would walk through hell for my son, every single day if I had to. Maybe every day is special simply because I remember the days when they weren't. Our bond is often remarked upon, and our similarities and shared sense of humour (God help him).

For a long time, Wolfgang used to put my kisses in his pocket. Sometimes I see him unconsciously still doing it. It is the cutest thing ever and a privilege reserved for me alone. Other times, however, he firmly puts me in my place. Once, dressed as Batman (as he regularly is), I was trying to get him to put his shoes on, again, we were late, again.

He looked me dead in the eye and said;

'Batman does not need shoes... and Batman does not need parents.'

I started laughing until I saw the look in his eye. My laughter died away. He was deadly serious. We were a bit quiet with each other after that. But I got over it. The little git laughs now when I tell him about it.

49

Captain Poo and Burger King

Before they are born, I like to believe that babies are like angels in the sky, looking out for their perfect mother.

When they find their perfect mother they choose her to deliver them into the world, love them and care for them. So each baby born has especially chosen that woman to become their perfect mother. I can't claim to own this story, I heard it somewhere, I can't remember, but it was so poignant that it really stuck in my mind and I would like to share it with you. It's important that you realise that you are enough. You are what the child needs and wants, exactly as you are. Wolfgang taught me that it's okay to use dry shampoo when you are too exhausted to wash your hair, that it's okay to wet wipe your black jeans before going to work. It's like he chose me anyway, despite my faults. I have never told him of my belief that babies choose their parents, and still he told me once, out of the blue, that he did choose me. So I like to believe it's true.

As a new mother, like I did, you might feel that you are the worst version of yourself. But remember, there are two tiny eyes who worship you already, who think you are perfect to them. Allow yourself to imagine that you might actually be doing better than you think. Trust those two little eyes. They think you are the very best version of yourself, their mother. Wolfgang definitely loves me, and thinks I am the best mother in the whole world. It is perhaps the most solid experience of being loved I have ever felt.

He tells me he loves me all the time and each time I smile and my chest hurts a little with love and pride.

However, he also pisses me off rather imaginatively. His favourite thing to call me recently - when I have put something healthy on his plate or asked him to get down from a frighteningly high wall is… Captain Poo. He says it really dramatically and often in his different accents, usually Scottish.

'Alright Captain Poo? How are you today?' it used to be funny but it's beginning to wear on me now. Especially in public.

I repay him with witty names of my own, a technique I'm pretty sure this won't be in any decent parenting book. It's like when he pisses me off I regress to being a child myself. You may have noticed my surname is King. Yes, so is Wolfgang's[31].

I was trying to have a nice mum and son 'date' in a ridiculously expensive café one afternoon after school. Coffee (as strong as cocaine and so hot I could barely sniff the steam), two tiny pieces of some sort of cake and some fancy pressed fruit juice for Wolfgang. When he realised that they didn't sell fricking fruitshoots, he exploded into a massive tantrum.

Oh no, hideously expensive and posh pressed fruit juice was not good enough for the little git. Twenty quid this ridiculous spread had cost me, I had romantic visions of the lovely photos we would get and the warm fuzzy feeling I would get when talking about Mum and son date. Naahhh. Course it didn't happen. Red faced with rage, he was flailing his arms around and swiped the glass of posh juice, knocking it over. The juice splattered everywhere, drowning our posh and very expensive brownies. I had been attempting my first sip of the steaming lava-like coffee and in shock at his actions accidentally took a massive swig. My mouth burned like the fires of hell, as I surveyed the damage.

---

[31] When I was considering writing this book, someone in the publishing field - honest to God, they really did - told me to pretend I was married to Stephen King, ensuring millions of book sales. Really they did. Sadly, I'm no relation to Stephen King. The closest I've ever come to having connections to famous people is the time me and Sleepless Beauty stalked Phil Mitchell from EastEnders around Manchester Airport once.

I lost it. I completely fucking lost it.

You know when you are out in public and you can't shout at your child? I tried to mop up the juice as my lips tried to turn inside out. Through gritted teeth and burned gums, (I still can't believe I did this) I told him that because he was being very naughty and whinging so much that I had changed his name, and that from now on he would be known as Burger.

I just don't know where it came from.

We left our expensive fare in the café and walked to the car. The penny dropped and he went completely ballistic. He screamed for thirty minutes that he wanted his old name back. He sobbed and sobbed and didn't believe me when I came to my senses after a few minutes, apologised and told him that I hadn't really changed his name. What an amazingly shit mother. Thankfully, we laugh about it now when we pass that particular restaurant.

'Eh Captain Poo, do you remember when you changed my name when I spilt that juice?' he will say.

'Yes, I remember, Burger King.'

He gives me a wink and a pretend scowl.

50
A Horse called Geoffrey

I haven't travelled completely unscathed through postnatal depression. Who knows, it might not be over yet for Captain Poo and her long-suffering Burger King. There is still a part of me who is desperate to be the perfect mother, desperate not to fail and convinced that I am not as good as the other mothers in the school yard. Ashamed when my complete failure at being a domestic goddess reveals itself by the slightly grey bits of polo shirt which poke out from beneath his jumper.

However, I now know when it's anxiety taking over logic. Just like the anxiety I help my clients with, the solutions are the same.

He *is* a normal kid and my occasional bursts of craziness and anxiety are just that, mine, not his.

At times he is feral, he is crazy, but he has morals. At six years old when I was finishing this, Wolfgang had developed an acutely sensitive reaction to right and wrong. I had to wrestle the laptop away from him after he noticed the word Bloody on the screen. He wore a disappointed-in-me look on his face.

'Mam, why is there swearing in Wolfgang's book?' he asked.

'Oh. Um. Because adults are kind of allowed to swear and it kind of makes adults laugh.'

He was disgusted with me and all other adults.

He regularly says mad things to me that I don't know how to respond to.

'Mam, you don't have a willy. I'll make you one out of this toilet roll.'

He goes mad when we brush his teeth and won't ever put his socks on or eat his meal in an appropriate timescale. But, I reckon that's pretty normal for his age. Aren't they all a bit mental?

But every day he tells me he loves me and his whole family, he brings me a special flower he has chosen regularly and in general is the goddamned most gorgeous little thing ever. And you know what, he can behave. Notice I say *can* rather than *does*. He can sit at a table and eat a meal, he can play nicely and he really cares about things. We have a secret hand squeeze and he can hold a polite conversation pretty well with a stranger. He loves his dog and has not tried to kill her yet.

The effect of postnatal depression may very well tell on our future relationship, and my son's attachment style may have been affected. But I can, with my whole heart say I did my best, I tried my hardest. This is all we can do. The guilt is powerful in how it makes us feel, but has little power to make things better. When we embrace our vulnerability, be kind to ourselves and make every effort to bond with our child so they experience a healthy attachment, now that kind of parenting is brave. In fact, experts in attachment tell us that children need to feel a rupture in their relationship in order to feel a repair. We need to feel the repairs so that we learn the rupture isn't permanent. So there is a little wisp of usefulness in those times where we completely lose our shit. I was so bloody relieved when I read about that. As a parent you really have to roll with the punches and celebrate all the little victories!

What is normal? I still panic about it. I am torn between furiously not caring about what normal means, appreciating the beautiful uniqueness of each child, to this occasional but fingernail-biting whisper in my head which regularly asks, but what if he's not? What if I have damaged him? What if I damage him by writing this… can you see the anxiety beginning to spiral again? I'm not sure if it will ever leave me truly, this idea that my influence on him is negative. But then he smiles at me and I can feel our connection and I relax.

Until those times where Wolfgang doesn't help my anxiety at all. Like me, he has a crazy imagination (and an impressive flair for coming up with insults). I'm not sure it's always a good thing. For example, a conversation we had just yesterday (as I write this we are just coming into September) went like this.

'Mam... is it nearly Christmas?' he asked hopefully.

'Well, it's a few months away still, chicken.' I replied.

'Can we start writing my list to Santa please?'

'Course we can, but it's a bit too early to send it off yet, and remember...'

'...I have to be a good boy!' he cuts across.

'That's right babe. So what do you want to write on your list?' I smile, wondering what toys I'm going to have to fork out for this year.

'I would like an eyeball popper and a horse called Geoffrey.'

'Uhh did you just say an eyeball popper...? And... a horse called Geoffrey...?'

'Yes, Mam,' he says as if these are the most normal things in the world to ask Santa for. As if I am the mad one.

It was one of the rare occasions that no response came out of my mouth. As we both vacantly stared at the tractor, my overactive imagination saw Wolfgang riding a smiling comedy horse, chasing people with some sort of torture tool designed to pop their eyeballs.

Never mind postnatal depression, Parenting in itself is a special sort of madness. It's just ridiculous sometimes. I wonder if he would be better off in the woods, being brought up by wild sheepdogs. At least he could rightfully be called *feral* then. Feral or not, I'd found the pot of gold at the end of the rainbow in my relationship with Wolfgang, which really makes my life worth living. The broken pieces of me which were just about glued together by a blond little angel boy called Wolfgang, who loved me so fiercely, and who never, ever let me go. He's the

215

tether that kept me from floating away and to this day we have the most astonishingly precious bond.

I would like to point out that his attitude towards swearing has fluctuated wildly over the years, the self-righteous little git. On holiday in Cyprus, he had just turned five, we were all eating at a restaurant when the waiter makes a comment about Wolfie's batman hat. Stavros - his name really was Stavros this is not a flippant stereotypical reference I've just thrown in there - asked him.

'What do you want to do when you grow up, little man?'

'I want to say swears!' was Wolfgang's reply. I just smiled at Stavros, pretending I hadn't heard.

51
Come on! Time for another?

I really began to enjoy being a mum. I found some peace, but sadly it was not to last. I was on medication for anxiety still at this point, so I didn't sink as deeply when things started going wrong again. I was also supported by a fiercely loving blond little angel on one side, and a dark handsome one on the other (don't tell him I said that either), who for some strange reason still seemed to love me despite the mania and the ongoing bowel issues!

When Wolfie was around four and was settled in school, people's opinions started changing from whispers to statements again. People (usually Scarys) had decided I needed their advice again.

'Isn't it time for Wolfgang to have a brother or sister to play with?'

'Two is just as easy as one!'

'Come on, time to have another one so he's not lonely!'

'Don't you think it's a bit mean to make him be an only child?'

I didn't want Wolfgang to be an only child. We are a very family orientated bunch and I adore my sister and brother. I wanted this for Wolfgang. But I had only just got better. I felt so selfish. Wolfgang's birth had been awful physically, and the couple of years afterwards had literally nearly killed me, my mental health had been so poor. And people expected me to do it again? I was in turmoil.

If I could have written a script for the next part of our lives it would have gone something like this.

When Wolfgang was four years old, Baby Lunatic and Fernando became pregnant again. Everyone was

217

ridiculously happy. Baby Lunatic's endometriosis symptoms had disappeared entirely and her pregnancy was trouble free. She gave birth naturally to a little girl in a birthing pool. In fact, she had the choice of three fucking birthing pools. Wolfgang was an amazing brother and Baby Lunatic floated through the early years of her daughter's life on a cloud of happiness and contentment. The four of them lived happily ever after. The End.

But of course, my life never works out like that.

As Wolfgang had grown, so had the endometriosis. To the backdrop of everyone telling me it was time for me to have another baby, unknown to most of them, I was still attending lots of medical appointments. At one time I had five different specialists. The endometriosis was developing rapidly. The gynaecology department at the hospital I attended even asked me if I would be willing to be a case study, as the disease was so advanced and widespread in my body. As well as the more typical endometriosis symptoms, I also had a much rarer form of it. I am very special because I have something called Extra-Pelvic Endometriosis. The medical community reckon it's very rare anyway, (in truth I reckon loads of people have got it, just that it is woefully misdiagnosed). As well as squatting in my pelvic cavity, this delightful disease was meandering its way around my bowel and into my diaphragm. They suspected it was already inside my lung. My bowel was being squeezed (a bit like the twist which separates one sausage from another), and the pain was having a severe effect on me.

Against the backdrop of all the medical appointments that people didn't know about, people continued reminding me of my obligation to give Wolfgang a brother or a sister. I learned that I had been lucky to conceive Wolfgang, because around this time I also learnt that one of the most common side effects of endometriosis is infertility.

52
Again?

My beautiful boy had survived my illness, both physically and, it seemed, emotionally. I hadn't killed myself, and I had realised with shock how grateful I was that thoughts of suicide had been fleeting, and unacted upon. The thought of leaving him, that I could have even thought of such a thing made me feel so upset. I was wholly there for him, and I would be until I drew my last breath. I had realised that this little angel wanted me, faults and madness regardless, he wanted me to be his Mam. It was a heady feeling that came on slowly from about two years after I had given birth to him. We were bonded, I had defeated the monster named Postnatal Depression.

I should have been elated, but I didn't have time for that. Because now I had another challenge I had to face.

I was terrified of having another baby.

I was terrified of not having another baby.

'Wolfgang needs a sibling! Don't be mean!' people said.

'Are you finished having children? We need to operate!' one surgeon said.

'Endometriosis causes infertility!' the research said.

'If you plan to try for another child, it's now or never!' another surgeon said.

Fuck, my brain said.

Having another child was an enormous decision for me, and not one I felt able to make so quickly. I felt as if I was being torn apart. Not only was I being pressurised to have a baby quickly because of my medical issues, I was also gripped with terror at the thought of having a baby and going through postnatal depression again. We were perfectly happy as we are, but a part of me longed for another chance, another chance to have a child and not develop postnatal depression, to attach in a more natural way. I longed to birth a child, to experience it as it is supposed to be, to give my son a sibling, a friend. To add to our family without trauma, poor mental health and self-hatred. The warrior in me who had recovered from postnatal depression baulked at the idea of risking it again. There was no way of knowing how it would be. There was no guarantee that just because I'd experienced birth trauma and postnatal depression that I would have it again, but there was also no guarantee I wouldn't. There was no promise that I would even be able to conceive a child again. What would it do to Fernando, never mind me, if we decided to try and then we couldn't have another baby?

53
Forced to Choose

For now, the excruciating choice in front of me was taken out of my hands, and the consequences of the choice I had to make would make my chances of having a baby slimmer.

At my next appointment, the colorectal surgeon told me that if my bowel was to become anymore diseased by the endometriosis, the consequences could be as severe as having to wear a colostomy bag for the rest of my life. They told me they had cut as much out of me as they dared. They told me that the only way for this disease to stop growing was to stop feeding it with my hormones. Which in practical terms, meant they were going to put me into the chemical menopause for six months. The issue with my bowel was so severe I had to make the decision whether to have the first injection there and then at that appointment. The surgeon was kind, but the clock was ticking. Once I'd had the first injection, it was likely my fertility will be lowered forever (on top of reduced fertility anyway), even if I decided to stop having the injections.

The other side of the pain and worry was that in order to try and avoid parts of my bowel dying and poisoning me, and worst case scenario, having to wear a colostomy bag, I had to inflict more hormonal chemicals upon my body, chemicals which are likely to affect my mental health, in the same way as giving birth did.

But I had no choice. Tears pouring down my face, I agreed to have the first injection. I lay down on the blue paper covered bench. They stabbed it into my belly, it was actually quite painful. I would have the rest of the injections at the GP.

The side effects hit me quickly. They were horrific and my mental health took a downwards spiral for a bit – again I was at the mercy of hormonal changes. At my next gynaecology appointment, the specialist told me that once this process was finished, it was my last chance to make my decision, because they needed to remove my ovaries. The name of this procedure is an Oophorectomy which is an ironically funny word for a rather unfunny thing. I was told that I could delay the ovary removal to try for a baby, although my fertility was likely to have been hugely impacted by the chemical menopause.

Making the decisions I had to make was unbearable. Fernando stood by me as he always had, not blaming me and supporting me. I could see he was gutted, although he didn't tell me that. I knew by now just how very lucky I was to have already conceived once, a huge proportion of women with this disease are unable to conceive. This was another reason I felt eternally guilty, with a similar feeling to how I imagine disaster survivors feel. I had managed to conceive. But everything had almost been completely fucked by having a traumatic birth and then postnatal depression.

Again, I was so afraid. I thought I was already beginning to lose myself. I wondered what part of me would die this time. My internal organs, my chance of having another child or my sanity? My marriage? Would Fernando get sick of the illnesses? Get sick of my infertility?

I had to walk through hell again, only this time without the shining beacon of love at the end of the process, just the final nail into the coffin of my chance to try again for a baby. To have a child and feel the joy.

But then - I would force myself to remember - I had survived it all so far. Maybe I could survive anything? Having a baby sapped my confidence. It really did. But having a toddler and a little boy gave it back (when he wasn't swearing in public, collecting used chewing gum or fighting with the dog). It was things like being woken up by a beautiful little boy who said I smelt like flowers, when I had assumed I smelt like death in the morning. I had a wonderful husband, who loved me best when I was taking the piss out of him, who supported me through thick and thin, whilst taking the piss right back at me. I had my boys, and they had me. We were already a family.

54
Kintsugi

Of course, I didn't want to tell you all of this. I didn't want to tell you about the horrible bits. I just wanted to take the piss out of Fernando, and tell you funny stories about my brilliant, feral child. But, as uncomfortable as it was, if I had avoided telling you about postnatal depression, if I had avoided telling you about endometriosis, I would be as guilty as the decision-makers who overlook the need to research and treat reproductive related illnesses and diseases in women, the medical experts who close their eyes to these massive issues and divert funding away from them.

I am aware that I have not painted a particularly good picture of myself. This is me. This is real. I had to share the shit bits. I hope to fly a flag for struggling mothers everywhere, the beautiful lunatics who have lost their space bar button. I know my family will shake their heads and hide their faces in disgust at my swearing and talking about vaginas, nipples, alcohol and all sorts of distasteful subjects.

But I don't really care.

I've already been through hell, nothing else can touch me surely? Can it? The future scares me, but not as much as the past.

Don't be fooled by me, please don't be fooled by my jokes. Layered between the sarcasm and the stories of the crazy things that happened, you can probably see bits of me that I still feel a bit scared to share. The bits of me that weren't okay. The parts of me, poisoned by postnatal depression until I felt like I was a monster. The bits of me that in my madness joked about paedophiles… I was certainly not myself. I disgusted myself. Shocked and ashamed at the weird shit coming out of my mouth.

Postnatal depression is an illness. But it doesn't feel like one, or at least it didn't to me. It felt like it was just me. Like I was just shit. Like I had failed something important. I blamed myself. Even as I began to surreptitiously consider I may have this postnatal depression thing, I still blamed myself. I blamed myself for getting it. I felt I was weak for succumbing to it. Ashamed. I felt I had caused all of this. I was completely lost. I just couldn't get past this feeling of otherness. This wasn't how it was supposed to be. Like all the other mothers that I think are out there, who believe themselves to be somehow not natural or normal. Like the other mothers who begin to believe that something terrible will happen to their babies, as some sort of punishment for them not being normal or a good enough mother. Because I now know I'm not alone, there are fucking loads of us. I now know it wasn't a reflection of who I truly was, or of my true feelings towards my baby right then. I can see now, that underneath the fear and the shame and the crippling anxiety, I absolutely adored him, with every molecule of my being. I wish I could somehow travel back in time and reassure the old me, give her a massive hug and maybe ~~tell her to stop eating so many custard creams~~ tell her that everything will be okay.

Because of my research I obviously knew a bit about postnatal depression, but never gave myself the benefit of thinking that that's what I was experiencing. Duh! Postnatal depression couldn't possibly be this mad shit going on in my head? Couldn't possibly be the reason for all this? It couldn't. No way. I was definitely a monster. I felt for everyone I had heard of or read about who had experienced postnatal depression. But not me. Not this. I was just purely a monster – this is how I felt when I couldn't accept that I had this illness. I felt like I didn't deserve to excuse what was wrong with me by naming it as a condition. That would mean it wasn't my fault. Of course it wasn't my fault. I realised eventually.

I was skilled at showing and feeling empathy and compassion for others, at the same time I showed myself absolutely no mercy. Before I gave birth, for hour after hour, day after day, week after week, month after month, for years and years I was non-judgemental and empathic to others. I humbly sat with them in their deepest, darkest places. But for some reason, I couldn't sit with myself, I couldn't help but judge myself so very, very harshly. Thankfully, with my own personal therapy and the help of my wonderful friends, I came to accept that my broken pieces were put back together. I was pulled out of the shit.

Kintsugi (Golden Joinery) is the Japanese art form of repairing items of broken pottery with precious metals like gold. As a philosophy, it treats breakage and repair as part of the history of an object, rather than something to disguise. I guess this philosophy applies very much to my experiences and sharing this stuff with you.

I used to feel cracked, broken. Now I feel threaded through with gold, and I wonder whether this latest occurrence will be another beautiful scar, or the catalyst that completely breaks me. I don't know yet if being threaded with gold is a good thing or not, I hope it is. I don't know what the future holds. I don't know what is going to happen to me. I wonder if I will be writing The Teenage Lunatic or The Menopause Lunatic from inside a padded cell, impervious to the stench of my colostomy bag. The occasional visit from Hosenose, Manykids, The Enforcer and Sleepless Beauty, their faces pitying and their noses wrinkled from my stinking helplessness.

It's not over. I have to keep going, colostomy bag or not. And I will. I'll keep going because Wolfgang needs me. And so do all the other littles that will come my way, with their trauma and pain.

Just tonight I was reminded of this, on both counts.

A lady phoned me tonight, out of the blue. She is around the same age as me and has a son the same age as Wolfie. She had got my phone number on the recommendation of another of my families.

There is no gentle way to say it. She has cancer, and her life is currently in the balance. If she responds to treatment over the next few days, there is a slim chance she might live. If she doesn't respond well, she will be moved to the palliative care ward. She wanted me to promise that I would provide support for her son should the worst happen. Which, she told me, is the most probable outcome.

Therapists shouldn't make promises. I don't usually, it isn't professional. But all that went out the window. A massive lump in my throat, I broke my own rule, and promised from one mother to another that I would help her son to heal when the time came.

And bar me being run over by a bus, I will keep this promise. My details are to be put to one side ready for her husband to contact me.

I have no words to describe how I feel about this. I bawled my eyes out after this call. As a self-employed person, obviously you have to think about finances, but I hope sincerely that I never make a single penny out of working with this family. I hope and pray she survives.

A part of me wonders where the hell my strength will come from in the future… But there is a bit of me that feels like I'm now immune to walking through fire. Because now I know I can. Because as I walk through the maddening maze that is my life, as well as the big pair of feet that have walked next to mine for the last two decades, my hand encased in a big warm strong hand, two little feet now walk on the other side of me, and a little hand gives mine our secret squeeze.

If life really is like a box of chocolates, to quote the wonderful Forrest Gump, I have selected my fair share of coffee and strawberry cream sweets (urgh, who even eats strawberry chocolate?). But it's really important for me to remember the toffees and the caramels too, like the people I am extremely lucky to have in my life, my family, my crazy friends, Fernando and of course, the star of this show, my Wolfgang. Lucky to have all the people who helped repair my cracks with gold.

Although I face this new challenge, I will remember what I achieved. I am his mother; he is my son. Just as it should be. I am not a Yummy Mummy, in fact I'm even not sure now if they exist....

I am proud.
I am Baby Lunatic.

Pubwatch has already decided that should I require a colostomy bag, we are going to design my whole outfits around it. She says we will accessorise it! Instead of something to hide, she thinks we should make a feature out of it... which is a pretty good metaphor for my life I think sometimes, glittering the colostomy bag instead of the actual turd.

So... if you ever come across a stinky woman with green eyebrows, sporting a sparkly colostomy bag and bickering furiously with her golden-haired teenager, taunting him by calling him 'Burger King', for God's sake please hand her a glass of gin, a wet wipe, a packet of chewing gum and then just keep fucking walking. Please don't judge her, she does enough of that herself.

The End.

Epilogue
24 things I wish in knew before I became a parent.

Don't be a judgy twat towards parents, it's hard enough for them as it is (I was guilty of this).

The Birth. Hope for peace, plan for war. Do not have a birthing plan, do take all the drugs.

Don't bother buying muslin squares.

Listen to your instinct, not your hormones. You got this.

You biologically know how to bond with your baby and keep them alive, and your baby knows how to bond with you.

Accept help, you really don't need to do everything and be everything.

Feed your baby, breast or bottle, as long as the job gets done. Maybe don't feed them Toffee Crisps.

Do not feel ashamed to bottle feed. Nope. Not allowed.

Your child is probably going to eat chicken nuggets whether you like it or not. And they might not eat cucumbers. Sorry.

Things are going to get weird. Feeling a bit weird for a couple of weeks after having a baby is normal, but any worse than weird, or any longer than a few weeks, you need to tell someone, because it's not normal and it's not just you.

If you don't get those fireworks of love when you first set eyes on your baby, don't beat yourself up – it will happen, but maybe a bit more slowly if you have had a traumatic birth.

If you do have to have a C-section, you will recover, despite the fact that you feel like you have been cut in half. The massive gash in your stomach will stick back together again, I promise.

If your mental health is suffering, do not be afraid to take medication if a doctor prescribes it. Do not be scared or ashamed, especially in traumatic birth situations, your brain might need some help to get over the chemical impact of trauma.

You are not going to automatically shit yourself in labour. I didn't. You're welcome.

Don't be friends with people just because you have a baby the same age. Having nothing else in common, it's going to be really hard to keep your identity. Keep your circle close, there are many knobheads out there!

But don't be afraid of making new friends either, do go to ~~Swimming for Hippos~~ pre-natal exercise classes. You might just meet your new best mate there. Look for the ones giving the midwife shit.

Having a baby might actually be the worst thing that ever happens to you.

*But having that particular baby might be the **best** thing that ever happened to you as well.*

A LOT of people bullshit about how well they are doing, how wonderful parenting is etc. Take it with a pinch of salt. I bet they are winging it too.

You don't need to buy a people carrier, or five different beds for your baby.

Everyone is going to have an opinion about babies, birth and parenting.

Even expert opinions conflict with each other. There is no one right way. Listen to everything, nod and thank them, and then do things your own way anyway.

If you experience a traumatic birth, don't pressure yourself to look back on that day and convince yourself it was the best day of your life. If you are experiencing post-traumatic stress symptoms, like flashbacks, intrusive thoughts or avoiding thinking about it, it's normal to respond like this, accept that you did go through a massively traumatic situation. Speak to your doctor, midwife or someone you trust.

There is help out there. If you feel that you might be experiencing post-natal ill health, you can get better, again, speak to your doctor, midwife or trusted people. If you don't feel like you can, there are some great organisations out there who can help you, you can find non-judgemental support at the following websites.

The Birth Trauma Association
A charity that supports women who have had a traumatic birth experience, or who are suffering from post-traumatic stress disorder (PTSD) after birth.
www.birthtraumaassociation.org.uk

PANDAS Foundation UK
Support and advice for any parent who is experiencing a perinatal mental illness.
0843 2898 401
www.pandasfoundation.org.uk

Unfold Your Wings
Supporting people affected by birth trauma and PTSD.
www.unfoldyourwings.co.uk

Thank you so much for reading my story. Sending big loves out to all my fellow lunatics and thank you for your support. Please leave me a positive review if you have enjoyed this and keep an eye out for my next projects please.

Follow me on social media to learn more about my ridiculous life and writing
Instagram @ charlie.king.author
Facebook @ charliekingauthorlunatic

You can also contact me directly (I'm not important enough to have my emails read by someone else unfortunately) at
charlie.king.author@icloud.com

CCK
x X x

Printed in Great Britain
by Amazon

83744635R10144